WOW!
Resumes for
Health Careers

Leslie Hamilton

McGraw-Hill

New York   San Francisco   Washington, D.C.   Auckland   Bogotá
Caracas   Lisbon   London   Madrid   Mexico City   Milan
Montreal   New Delhi   San Juan   Singapore
Sydney   Tokyo   Toronto

Library of Congress Cataloging-in-Publication Data

Hamilton, Leslie [date].
    WOW! resumes for health careers   / Leslie Hamilton.
        p.   cm.
    Includes index.
    ISBN 0-07-026028-1
    1. Resumes (Employment)   2. Medical personnel—vocational
guidance.   I. Title.
    R690.H35   1998
    650.14—dc21   98-27257
                                                                                      CIP

McGraw-Hill

*A Division of The **McGraw·Hill** Companies*

1 2 3 4 5 6 7 8 9 0 MAL/MAL 9 0 3 2 1 0 9 8

ISBN 0-07-026028-1 (pbk.)

*The sponsoring editor for this book was Betsy Brown, the assistant
editior was Kurt Nelson, the editing supervisor was Fred Dahl, and the
production supervisor was Clare Stanley. It was set in Stone Serif by
Inkwell Publishing Services.*

Printed and bound by Malloy Lithographics, Inc.

McGraw-Hill books are available at special quantity discounts to
use as premiums and sales promotions, or for use in corporate
training sessions. For more information, please write to the
Director of Special Sales, McGraw-Hill, 11 West 19th Street, New
York, NY 10011. Or contact your local bookstore.

Dedication

To my family

Contents

Alphabetical Listing of Resumes

Acknowledgments

My gratitude goes out to the many people who helped me to turn this book into a reality, including my editor Betsy Brown, who showed patience and support throughout the process; my friends Brandon Toropov and Glenn KnicKrehm, who offered important insights from the business world; Judith Burros, whose administrative and moral support was always extraordinary; Bert Holtje, who, directly and indirectly, gave me hope to carry on; my husband Bob, without whom the book would never have come into existence; and my three daughters Meghan, Emma, Cassie, now as always inspirations to their mother.

Leslie Hamilton

About the Author

Leslie Hamilton (Boston, MA) is a writer and researcher who has written and contributed to numerous books in the areas of careers and personal finance.

Introduction

The "Hmmm..." Factor

Wow! Resumes for Health Careers is dedicated to the proposition that you can't win a job offer if nobody ever bothers to read your resume.

Your resume isn't—or, at any rate, shouldn't be—a dry, quasi-legal document (or, for that matter, an excuse to exaggerate your capabilities). It is—or, at any rate, ought to be—an advertisement that stops readers in their tracks and makes them long to find out more about you.

To the extent that your resume brings you closer to this ideal, it will be successful; to the extent that it leaves people thinking, "Gee, this one really doesn't look much different from any of the others," it will fail.

This book features guidelines, examples, and checklists meant to help you make your resume stand out. Each chapter examines a particular resume challenge, highlights strategies you can use to make your resume stand out from the crowd, and offers sample resumes meant to help you fashion a resume that will help you win the numbers game and get the interview and, eventually, the job offer you deserve.

When employers review resumes and job queries, their thinking process goes something like this: "What a huge stack of resumes. I don't know how I'm ever going to get through this one. Oh, well, better get started. Let's see. No. No. No. No. No. No. No. No. No. [Pause] Hmmmmmm..."

"Hmmm..." means an interview. It means a chance to shine in person and to win the offer you deserve.

> **KEY POINT:**
>
> Your resume's job is to win the battle of the declining attention span and generate something akin to "Hmmm..." from a decision maker.

In this book, you'll find strategies and over 100 model resumes that will help turn no into "Hmmm" and, finally, into yes.

1

The Health Care Hiring Game

What Top Hiring Officials Want To See—and What They Don't

In creating, the only hard thing's to begin; a grass-blade's no easier to make than an oak.

JAMES RUSSELL LOWELL

Sometimes, simply following "the rules" is the worst way to go.

Take the task of finding a job within the health care field. Although following established procedure makes the most sense when it comes to *fulfilling the responsibilities* of countless jobs in the field, it's not necessarily the best way to get the attention of a hiring official. Like just about everyone else these days, the people who make decisions about whether to hire you are pretty busy. They need more than a factual recitation. They need to hear about realistic potential solutions to the difficult problems they face every day.

Peter F. Drucker recently wrote a piece in *The Wall Street Journal* (March 29, 1995) that touched on this topic. Drucker's remarks are worth reviewing here:

"Most resumes I get ... list the jobs the person has held," Drucker wrote. "A few then describe the job the person would like to get. Very few even mention what the person has done well and can do well. Even fewer state what a future employer can and should expect from that person. In other words, very, very few people look upon themselves as a 'product' that must be marketed."

KEY POINT

As a practical matter, you probably *shouldn't* expect a resume that obediently lists every position you've ever but, and does little else, to get superior results for you.

What Drucker is calling for, I believe, is a completely different type of resume than the one many of us are accustomed to writing or reading—the kind that makes hiring officials break their routine and say "Hey, wait a minute!" or, better yet, "WOW!"

The objective, then, is to formulate a WOW resume. This is a resume that takes responsibility, not simply for listing job titles, but also for supplying information about what the person has done well and can do well.

Aggressively highlighting possible solutions to the problems decision makers face on a daily basis is, in my view, the only intelligent approach to resume development in today's employment market. What follows is some practical advice on developing such a WOW resume, and examples you can use as you craft your own.

What Decision Makers Want to See

An informal canvassing of insiders familiar with medical hiring decisions at companies large and small resulted in some intriguing what-they're-looking-for insights from prospective employers. Take a look at the following selections that appeared on the "Hot Job Listings" section of Pam Pohly's Healthcare Home Page (<http://www.pohly.com/jobs.html>).

- "Seeking experienced hospital administrators with track records in turnarounds, marketing, team building, strategic planning."

- "Prefer individual with referral development and account management experience in managed care, acute care hospital, or psychiatric hospital setting."

- "Currently searching for Hospital Marketing Directors, Managed Care Contractors, Community Service Reps, and Account Managers."

- "Seeking an experienced individual with hospice experience. BSN required, MSN preferred. Management experience and home health experience important."

- "Board specifically seeking mature individual with proven people skills, solid integrity, and track record in establishing and sustaining employee morale and team productivity. Equanimity under stress and long-range focus are attributes for the chosen leader walking into this exciting but complex reorganization. Sophistication in managed care business development, service line matrix organization, physician relations, and rural outreach important. Masters degree and RN required, MSN preferred."

Although these openings appear to have no common thread, most of the positions listed have very specific requirements. Only one listing mentions general characteristics such as people skills and integrity, and these general traits are included in a long list of well-defined skills and expected areas of competency.

Your most important guideline in assembling your WOW health care resume, then, should probably be:

• Make sure that your abilities match the job requirements!

Many skills simply do not transfer easily from one health care concentration to another, and in all but the lowest-level entry positions in health care, the employer is looking for very specific skills to fill a very specific job. If you don't have those skills, you should rethink your job search objectives.

The following quote is from a job listing at a major urban medical center, circulated while the employer was seeking a "customer-focused individual to provide analytical support in compensation."

The Medical Center of Central Georgia is a dynamic and progressive 518-bed hospital employing more than 3,500 employees and serving a 52-county area in Central and South Georgia. We are currently seeking a results-oriented, customer-focused individual to provide analytical support in compensation. Responsibilities include conducting market analysis, completing salary surveys, providing analytical support for job evaluation and analysis, writing job descriptions, and assisting the HR team in maintaining the classification and compensation plans. Qualifications: BS in business or related field; 3 years of progressive "hands-on" compensation experience, preferably in the health care industry. Proficiency in Microsoft Office software spreadsheets and databases is essential, as well as the ability to communicate effectively with all levels of the organization. Mainframe HR/payroll system experience desirable.

As this ad suggests, the market is large enough and diverse enough that employers can search for, and find, employees with the precise qualifications desired.

The health care industry is very image conscious, and many listings place an emphasis on high-tech programs and state-of-the-art facilities. Another urban medical facility provides an example of this kind of recruiting appeal:

Building the Technology for Tomorrow. On May 23, 1998, (we) will open our new $65-million, 390,000-square-foot medical center that will certainly set us apart from our contemporaries.... In "Building the Technology for Tomorrow," this complex will include state-of-the-art diagnostic, imaging, monitoring, information-system, and invasive capabilities that will—not only reinforce our mission and vision of providing quality, cost-effective health care service—but will also complement the pride we take in providing excellent patient care. But that isn't enough! We are seeking eager, qualified, competent, and focused R.N. staff who will allow us to invest in their future as they invest in ours—while we, in turn, combine forces to invest in the future of our culturally diverse community and the population we serve. Bring your skills, education, experience, and desire to expand your nursing career to our rapidly growing medical center and let us provide you a wonderful opportunity for professional training and growth in the latest state-of-the-art health care environment.

A second important guideline in developing an effective health care resume might be:

• Present yourself and your skills in accordance with the "state-of-the-art-community" image your potential employer wishes to present.

In many cases, this means acquiring or updating technology-specific training, and highlighting the ways in which you are "eager, qualified, competent, and focused" when it comes time to use these skills.

Cultural diversity and minority participation also affect the overall picture of job openings and hiring practices within the health care industry. If you are seeking a job in any of the principal population centers of the United States, multilingual skills are an exceedingly valuable asset, and should figure prominently on your resume. But no matter where you are seeking a job, sensitivity to cultural diversity is critical.

Medsearch (<http://www.medsearch.com>) is a large and diverse website devoted to finding jobs in the field of medicine. Medsearch lists four principal subcategories on its home page, and one of them is cultural diversity. The prominent placement afforded to cultural diversity is evidence of the importance of the issue. Recruitment and retention of qualified minorities remains an important issue in the industry; underrepresentation of minorities in the health professions is recognized as a major problem.

So a third important guideline is:

- Present your assets clearly in the area of cultural diversity and sensitivity.

If you are a member of a racial minority, bear in mind that that fact may enhance your appeal. You may be able to increase your chances of success on the job front by *tactfully and subtly* listing affiliations or school activities that help to identify your status. (You might, for instance, decide to list your membership in your college's African-American Student Council in a single discreet but noticeable line at the bottom of your resume.) If you have language skills or other demonstrable assets in the area of cultural diversity, make sure your resume highlights them appropriately.

The health care job market is so broad that there is little reason to apply for jobs that don't match your expertise or experience. If you have some relevant experience in the right employment category, and if you persevere (and are comfortable considering relocating for the right opportunity), there's a very good chance that you'll be able to find a position that matches your skills and goals. The bottom line is this: assuming you have skills, training, and some experience in a relevant health care field, and assuming you can use your resume to broadcast key messages like the ones identified in this chapter, you should be able to find a job that fits what you have to offer and advances your personal goals.

Fortunately, the health care field appears poised for continued expansion. On the Bureau of Labor Statistics' "25 Occupations that Have the Highest Median Weekly Earnings Requiring a Bachelors Degree or Higher," six are specifically health-related careers, and ten more are in the areas of management and administration, which overlap with the health care field. Similarly, among the "25 Fastest-Growing Occupations from 1994 to 2005," 11 are specifically health-related careers, and another 5 are in the areas of administration and management.

Your resume will stand or fall on its ability to broadcast your capacity for achievement. In most cases, this broadcasting is done through creative use of a number of basic elements, including a heading with pertinent contact information; a "grabber" introductory section (perhaps either a professional summary or a targeted objective of direct interest to a particular employer); an extensive employment section outlining responsibilities, skills, and accomplishments; and a brief overview of your educational qualifications.

In addition, you may wish to add a separate category at or near the end of your resume, one I call the Hey-look-me-over element. Traditionally, the end of the resume has been reserved for headings such as "Other" or "Personal"—with the unfortunate result that applicants have used the bottoms of their resumes to talk about their fondness for checkers or the names of their pets. *Striking* and *directly relevant* material should show up in the Hey-look-me-over section— information or insights that define you as a person and a potential employee. You may decide not to use this final element. However, the final portion of your resume offers you a great chance to set yourself apart from other candidates— and that's the name of the game.

An in-depth discussion of the core purposes of your resume follows in Chapter 2.

Creative Pestering

Before we move on, let me leave you with another important piece of job search advice. Taking responsibility for the job search yourself, rather than ceding it to, say, the personnel department, makes all the difference in your results. I call this *creative pestering*.

Should you really *pester* prospective employers? Well, yes, but only in a very limited sense of the word. By *pester*, I don't mean be a pest but, rather, continually find the nicest possible ways to get yourself onto people's to-do lists.

Creative pestering *doesn't* mean ...

- Leaving indignant or annoying messages on voice mail systems
- Taking an attitude with receptionists and administrative support staff

KEY POINT

The applicant who finds the most creative, persistent ways to pester is usually the one who gets the offer.

- Appearing combative or adversarial during an interview
- Pulling crazy stunts that are likely to get you thrown out of the joint (like the overbearing applicant who decided to camp out in the president's office until the top banana agreed to meet with him personally)
- Wearing down key decision makers by declaring some kind of personal vendetta against the target company

Creative pestering *does* mean ...

- Doing the research necessary to make proposals and suggestions that benefit the hiring official—for free
- Following every apparent no with a question about future hiring patterns and staying in touch with decision makers who've turned you down to ask about new hiring initiatives
- Proposing intelligent part-time contract assignments on your own initiative
- Offering to buy decision makers an early breakfast to get the latest information on hiring within the company or industry
- *Making countless pleasant phone calls* (that "pleasant" part is vitally important) in order to develop or learn more about professional opportunities

The model resumes that appear in this book will forward your candidacy in an effective, persuasive way. When combined with a strategy of creative, persistent pestering, they will help you land that great job you deserve.

2

Some Resume Basics
What the Resume Is Meant to Do

The greatest truths are the simplest.
J.C. AND A.W. HARE

The reason most resumes don't fall into the WOW category is simple: most people who write resumes have serious misconceptions about what, exactly, a resume is meant to do. What is the purpose of this ubiquitous document? What's it meant to accomplish? What are the objectives of writing one? What *shouldn't* a resume be expected to do? Once you resolve these questions, you'll be in a much better position to craft a resume that makes the decision maker stop and say, "WOW!"

What a Resume Isn't

A resume is not ... an application for a position. Prepare yourself for a shock: the vast majority of resumes are completely ignored. In fact, so many resumes are sent "blind" to decision makers that the act of popping one in the mail, doing nothing beforehand or afterwards, amounts to little more than an exercise in wishful thinking. That brings us to (sigh) the bubble-burst of the day: *putting your resume into the mail does not, in and of itself, represent a meaningful form of outreach to a potential employer.* In fact, a fair number of experienced career counselors warn strongly that a resume should *never* be mailed, period. Instead, they counsel, a superior *letter* (like the models that appear in Chapter 3) is a better initial form of outreach for making, and eventually telephoning, new contacts.

KEY POINT

No matter what you may read or hear to the contrary from the prospective employer, you really shouldn't think of yourself as having applied for a job if you haven't talked to someone within the company about it. For most employment settings, the don't-mail-the-resume advice is pretty solid. You're far better off putting together a punchy written appeal that makes your cold call to a decision maker at a target company just a little warmer—or calling existing members of your own network and developing new contacts and leads in that way. To paraphrase the Beatles, mailing out resumes without any personal contact is a bit like trying to get a tan by standing in the English rain.

Once you've established some kind of relationship with the contact at your target company, *then* you can make arrangements for an in-person meeting, formal or informal. That's the time to pass along a *version of* your resume that makes sense for the opening in question. And, yes, a well-structured letter, like the ones that appear in this book, can help you overcome the send-in-your-resume-and-then-we'll-talk trap so familiar to people who make job-related networking calls. All the same, I recognize that the temptation to send a resume and see what happens can be incredibly strong. Because a few (and I do mean very few) situations require you to send a "blind" resume and cover letter, you'll want to take a look at the discussion of these situations that appears in the next chapter.

A resume is not … a single document you can write once and consider finished. Please *don't* make the time-consuming mistake of believing that a job search consists of developing a single resume, finding advertised openings, and mailing out copies of it until something happens. Instead, get on the phone with friends and associates, send out letters to new prospective employers (see Chapter 3), and *target* each resume you send out. By doing so, you'll set yourself apart from the pack. It's certainly true that not many people actually *like* writing resumes. Most people want to write the resume once and mail it to 50 different employers. That probably explains why these documents so rarely have any direct bearing on the employment openings they're supposed to help applicants track down.

The resume you pass along to a decision maker should be focused specifically on the company and/or position in question. A fair number of the sample resumes that follow in this book take the perfectly reasonable, and entirely accurate, step of listing as the objective the specific job the job seeker is pursuing at that particular company. This course of action is much sounder than stating your objective from your own perspective (e.g., to locate a position within a dynamic firm that will allow me to grow professionally). That you should be ready to use your computer to customize, not only a single line, but all essential elements of your resume's text, is taken here as a given. *Learn what problems the decision maker is hoping to resolve, and then focus your resume on those problems!*

A resume is not ... an affidavit. It's an advertisement, a marketing tool, a device that must use every (accurate!) statement it possibly can to forward your candidacy.

The right resume information is that which inspires the decision maker to pursue your candidacy further—and any sample resume you encounter, including those that appear in this book, should be considered a *suggested* format for adaptation to the specific situation you face.

What a Resume Is

A resume is ... something meant to be scanned. Long, dense blocks of type have a way of turning hiring officials off—although in certain situations they can serve you well by amplifying points specifically raised by the prospective employer earlier in the process.

Most (though not all) of the resumes that appear in this book feature condensed "talking points" rather than long essays on particular aspects of one's work experience. There's a reason for taking this approach—*virtually no one reads resumes,* at least not in the early stages of your contact with the target company. Expect your resume to be scanned quickly, not studied minutely.

A resume is ... a convenience for the hiring official. Shocking news! The resume is really a way to screen you out of the organization. That's right—the decision maker typically uses your resume to make more or less instantaneous yes-or-no determinations about your candidacy—and the candidacies of literally hundreds of other applicants. Employers almost always have a big pile of resumes from potential applicants. The hiring official has to make that pile disap-

KEY POINT

It means you may have only a few seconds—perhaps a few *fractions* of a second—to make or reinforce a positive impression with the resume you create.

pear, and so almost always uses resumes to find out what *doesn't* match his or her requirements. That saves time that would otherwise have to be devoted to countless face-to-face discussions with eager applicants.

You have to make sure your "grabber" introductory material really does grab! And, since people tend to zip to the bottom of the page, you have to make sure that the Hey-look-me-over text you select to close your resume reinforces the message, "This one looks interesting." Within the body of the resume, you have to isolate benefits and make the reader awfully curious about finding out more in a hurry! And speaking of curiosity ...

A resume is ... an opportunity for you to leave the reader wanting to learn more. Insofar as the resume serves as a silent spokesperson in your absence, it must, like any good advertisement, eventually inspire your audience to action. In most cases the outcome you're after is a simple one: you want the person to pick up the telephone and either offer you the job or ask you to come in and discuss the job in detail. The objective is not to supply a full-blown professional biography, but to supply *enough telling facts* to make a decision to contact you easy to justify. After all, you'll want to save some of the heroics for your face-to-face discussion with your contact!

Now that you've gotten a good idea of what your resume is supposed to do, you're ready for ...

Twenty Big Questions That Will Help You Develop Your "Wow" Resume

Here are 20 questions to ask yourself about your own work history and education. Find a place where you can devote *at least 90 uninterrupted minutes* to the development of written answers to each of these questions. That's five to seven minutes per question. Jot down your answers in a looseleaf notebook. Give your best-guess answers for now. Be honest, and don't let yourself get bogged down in technical detail. If you find yourself thinking that answering a question fully requires some in-depth research on your part, leave that aspect of the question blank for now and make a note to come back to it later. For now, get the broad outlines to your answers for each of the Big Twenty.

1. What are the three most dramatic examples of verbal or written praise you've ever received from any supervisor or client? What awards, commendations, or formal acknowledgments have you received in any work setting?

2. What was the most recent job you held? (If you're presently employed, this will be your current job.) List the most important duties.

3. What skills do you have or did you have to develop to deliver superior results on the job in that environment?

4. Think of at least three situations when *failing* to do something you did in that work environment would have resulted in disaster for your employer. How much money, time, and resources would have been required to rectify the problem?

5. Think of at least three times a supervisor in this position outlined a problem for you to solve—a problem you *did* solve successfully. What was the positive outcome of each of those solutions? Did you make a system or procedure run more smoothly? If so, how much more smoothly? Did you save money? If so, how much money? Did you save time? If so, how much time?

6. Think of at least three instances when you personally "saved the day" as part of your work on this job—perhaps by thinking quickly in an emergency or acting responsibly during trying circumstances. Did a computer ever crash, leaving you to pick up the pieces? Was a customer ever angry over something you were able to resolve? Was a deadline ever moved up to a date that seemed impossible, but wasn't?

7. Answer question 2 for your next most recent job.

8. Answer question 3 for this job.

9. Answer question 4 for this job.

10. Answer question 5 for this job.

11. Answer question 6 for this job.

12. Answer question 2 for the job you held before that.

13. Answer question 3 for this job.

14. Answer question 4 for this job.

15. Answer question 5 for this job.

16. Answer question 6 for this job.

17. Write down the specifics of at least *five* situations where coworkers came to you for help and you were able to provide it. What was the worst-case scenario that was averted by your taking action? What positive outcome emerged instead?

18. Make a list of any extracurricular activities you may have pursued in school that provided you with experience that either *directly* related to the position you'd like to win or required you to develop significant leadership skills.

19. Make a list of any charitable activities that directly relate to the position you'd like to win.

20. Make a list of at least 15 people—former employers, colleagues, professional associates—who would be willing to develop short written recommendations for you, or to agree to endorse a recommendation you composed.

As you peruse the resumes in this book, you'll find that most of them make use of the kind of information the foregoing questionnaire asks you to develop. By taking time now and devoting a good, solid 90 minutes to answering the questions *in writing,* you'll put yourself in a position to highlight what employers really want to see: potential answers to pressing problems!

In the resume you develop using the models that appear in this book, you'll be able to provide the potential answers to those pressing problems in the form of ...

Compelling (legitimate!) endorsements from third parties

Examples of performance that saved time or money or increased efficiency

Instances when you took the initiative and forestalled disaster

Those are the kinds of resume elements that make for WOW resumes. There are dozens of examples of these types of items in the pages that follow, but take the time now to develop the material that puts you in the best possible light.

There Are References and There Are References

By the way, I should note here that some resume-writing authorities take a dim view of *attaching* written references to your resume on separate sheets of paper. I suppose I'd have to agree—this tactic looks a little desperate, and it's all too easy for the separate endorsements to become separated from your resume. (My experience is that a good many managers resent anything that adds to the clutter on their crowded desks.) A better approach is to *incorporate* the highlights of written or spoken endorsements—which can be a very powerful tool indeed.

In Chapter 4, you'll find a couple of brief, helpful checklists—summaries of resume and employment letter commandments, if you will. Those lists will help you evaluate your written appeals and make them as sharp as can possibly be. For now, take the time to answer the Big Twenty questions *in detail*. That work is the foundation of any attempt you'll make later to develop a superior resume based on the samples in this book.

Please *do not* continue on to the next portion of this book until you've completed the questionnaire work in this chapter.

Use Resume Models for Job Search Success

In this book are dozens of examples of superior resumes that will help you to take the raw material you develop by means of the foregoing questionnaire and develop your own WOW resumes. As you examine them, be prepared to adapt elements from more than one sample resume. Use what works. Use what makes sense for your situation.

KEY POINT

Adapt the formats of appropriate resumes—whether they follow a chronological format that examines dates of employment, a functional outline that emphasizes key skills of interest to *a particular reader,* or a combination of the two—with an eye toward making a dramatic, confident, positive impression on your reader.

When You Get Stuck

It happens to the best of us. Sometimes you run dry while you're working on your masterpiece of aggressive employment self-promotion. Don't panic. Find a constructive way to get around your roadblock.

Here are two strategies to consider when you find yourself staring at that long, blank sheet of white paper while setting up your initial notes— or, if you've finished your initial questionnaire and are transferring your work into a more polished form on your personal computer, that insistent cursor keeps blinking whether or not you've got something interesting to say.

Strategy One

Take a short break. Get up for a minute or two to grab a drink of water or pop a high-energy tape or CD onto the nearest music system. Most cases of writer's block come when we're pushing ourselves unreasonably, trying to turn out something when our minds have been on the case for too long. As long as you don't use the drink-of-water routine as an excuse to allow your stretches of constructive work to disintegrate into a four-minutes-on, two-minutes-off charade, you can usually get further by allowing yourself a modest break between (for instance) 15- or 20-minute time slots of work. When you hit a wall, find a way to clear your mind. Don't just keep demanding new results from the same exhausted brain cells. (Also, if you've just taken a short break and you're still stuck, move on to another section of your resume, and come back a little later on to the problem that has you stumped.

Strategy Two

Use a "superstar verb" for inspiration. The most powerful parts of your resume will be sentences that begin with active, results-oriented verbs (for example, "maintained 99.85% error-free contact database for use by sales force"). Here's a list of over 130 such verbs—play a little game with yourself and find 10 sentences that describe your own work background, each of which begins with a verb that addresses the area where you're stuck.

Superstar Verb List

accepted (responsibility, heavy workload, challenge, etc.)	accomplished
acted to ...	acted as troubleshooter for ...
adapted	adjusted

administered

advised

allocated

analyzed

appraised

approved

arranged

assembled

assigned

audited

authored

authorized

balanced

briefed

budgeted

built

calculated

catalogued

chose

clarified

coached

compiled

computed

conducted

consolidated

convinced

coordinated

critiqued

customized

cut

decreased

demonstrated

designed

determined

developed

devised

diagnosed

directed

dispatched

drafted

edited

eliminated

established

estimated

evaluated

executed

explained

facilitated

forecasted

formulated

found

founded

headed up

hired

identified

implemented

improved

increased

informed

initiated

inspected

installed

instituted

instructed

interpreted

interviewed

invented

launched

learned

led

managed

monitored

negotiated

organized

overhauled

planned

prepared

produced

promoted

publicized

qualified

reached out

reconciled

recruited

researched

reviewed

rewrote

scheduled

selected

shaped

simulated

solidified

specified

strategized

strengthened

supervised

systematized

trained

turned around

wrote

lectured

limited

marketed

motivated

operated

originated

oversaw

predicted

prioritized

programmed

prospected

published

reached

recommended

recorded

redesigned

resolved

revitalized

saved

screened

set

showed

sold

solved

spoke

streamlined

summarized

surveyed

toured

trimmed

upgraded

3

The Supporting Players

The Lowdown on Letters

Invention breeds invention.
RALPH WALDO EMERSON

Many people are surprised to learn that the look and feel of one's written job search material can have a surprisingly powerful impact on the final decision maker. Rest assured—it's true!

I strongly suggest that you coordinate your written job search correspondence by picking a particular, striking set of stationery and sticking to it throughout your correspondence with target companies. The paper you choose doesn't have to be expensive or visually overwhelming (in fact, it probably shouldn't be either), but it should broadcast professionalism in a consistent, understated way.

When the time comes to make a final decision about a new hire, the odds are good that your contact within the organization will make a final review of the written correspondence received from all applicants. How much do you think it will aid your cause for that decision maker to see that your resume, and the series of letters that accompany it, all share the same tasteful color scheme and basic look? This may seem like a small consideration, but believe me, paper selection can make a difference. (So can the decision to type or word process all your letters if your handwriting isn't exactly the world's neatest.)

I've already spoken a little bit about the dangers of mailing your resume. Let's examine this point in a little greater depth as it relates to the alternative we'll be discussing in this chapter—preresume letters.

There are three main points to bear in mind when you pop your resume into the U.S. mail:

1. Secretaries and administrative assistants routinely screen out unsolicited resumes. As a general rule, they're paid to do so! That means that *no matter what you say in the cover letter,* there's a very good chance that someone other than your intended recipient is going to spot the resume and put your correspondence aside for "later review." You know how often *you* get to the business correspondence you set aside for "later review"? That's about how often hiring officials will make it over to scan your resume.

2. Secretaries and administrative assistants virtually *never* know the difference between a resume that someone has asked to see and a resume that's been sent cold. They may spot your "as requested" notation—then again, they may not.

3. Secretaries and administrative assistants *don't* screen most personalized business-related correspondence. If your correspondence does *not* include a resume, it stands a much better chance of making it through to its intended recipient, especially when you're contacting employers about something other than advertised openings.

What does this all add up to? *Mailing resumes blind is, statistically speaking, more likely than not to be a waste of time, effort, and money.* On the other hand, sending a broadcast letter—a souped-up letter that offers more pertinent detail about your career than an untargeted letter, but less than a resume—is likely to mean that a decision maker actually sees what you've written.

Are there *some* situations in which you'd be well advised to send a resume and a top-notch cover letter? Sure. The hiring official may be located in another city and may demand to see a resume before asking you to fly out to discuss an opening. The hiring official may have lost the original copy of your resume that you delivered in person or may have asked you to develop a new version of your resume—and may simply refuse to meet with you personally until he or she has had the opportunity to review it.

In these cases you'll need to assemble a superior cover letter, one similar in impact to the samples that follow. But in *most* situations, your best course of action will be to make virtually any excuse that allows you to *speak* to your contact

KEY POINT

If you do opt to send a resume through the mails, *never* send one without a sharp-looking cover letter on matching stationery.

before delivering your resume in person. The resume you hand off should be targeted *directly* to the needs, requirements, and specifications of the employer with whom you've spoken.

One more important word of advice—think twice before you get overly creative in establishing a means of connection between your contact person and your resume or letter. No doubt this advice is familiar by now, but it bears repeating: try your level best to find some way to hand the package over yourself, during a face-to-face meeting. Such a strategy is far more effective than coming up with some elaborate delivery system designed to get the decision maker to pay close attention to your resume.

Overnight delivery services, bicycle couriers, flowers, gifts, oversized boxes, registered mail—believe me, seasoned hiring officials have seen it all, and they're more likely to wonder what you're trying to compensate for than they are to be impressed by your ingenuity. Take the money you were going to spend on renting a marching band or a small jet plane and put it back into your bank account. Set aside another hour or two to make sure the material that's on your resume tells a dramatic, confident story—and does so in a way that's immediately accessible to the reader.

The "Perfect" Letter

So—how do you use written materials to pave the way for a relationship with a contact within your target industry? Here's the single best tool I know of. This letter may not be "perfect," but it's pretty darned close. It shows that you've done your research, and that you're willing to take responsibility for cheerleading your own candidacy through the organization. It should be no surprise to you by now that I advocate sending this letter *without* a resume and following up by phone; however, you should know that the model can also serve as a superior cover letter on those rare occasions when you need to use it as one. Just add the sentence "My resume is enclosed." to the beginning of the paragraph before "Yours truly."

(Date)

John Miller
ABC Medical Equipment Center
456 Main Street
Mytown, State 00000

Dear Mr. Miller:

Jane Owens, in your Human Resources Department, tells me that you're looking for a Senior Widget Inventory Management Specialist.

ABC's Requirements	*Jane Smith's Experience*
College degree	Bachelor's degree in Widgeting from Worcester University, 1984
Two years experience with WidgetManager inventory control software	Six years experience with Widget-Manager inventory control software
Four years experience in a widget industry environment	Six years experience in a widget industry environment with American Widget
Knowledge of widget industry fulfillment patterns	Knowledge of widget industry fulfillment patterns
Familiarity with basic spreadsheet applications	6 years experience with spreadsheet programs including Excel and Lotus 1-2-3

I think we should talk about the ways I could make a significant contribution to ABC Medical Equipment Center. I look forward to speaking with you soon.

Yours truly,

Jane Smith
123 Main Street
Mytown, State 00000
(555) 555-5555

P.S. I will plan on calling you at 9:00 A.M. on Tuesday, July 16th. If this is not a convenient time, please tell Robin a better time for me to call.

This simple letter—which requires that you do a little phone research to determine the nature of the open position and the name of the receptionist, secretary, or administrative assistant—is the single most effective weapon in your arsenal when it comes to making contact with decision makers. That's not to say that it's guaranteed to get you an enthusiastic return call—no letter will always do that. But it *is* virtually certain to capture the interest and attention of anyone who reviews the mail, say, once a week, and has a vague appreciation of the fact that his or her organization is looking to hire a widget inventory specialist.

When you follow up by phone as promised, you're likely to hear a thoughtful pause and the rustle of paper as your contact searches for that intriguing letter that crossed the desk a few days back. That's what you want to hear. When your contact fishes the document out of the pile, find an opportunity to ask repeatedly and politely for an in-person meeting to discuss the position and, if time allows, ask the person what he or she is trying to get accomplished in the area you're interested in. Odds are you'll get some meaningful feedback—and some inspiration on the best way to target your resume for the meeting.

The beauty of the two-column approach is that you *focus only on matches between what you offer and what the prospective employer wants.* You don't bore the reader with your life story, and you don't supply lots of details that don't fit into the "right profile" the hiring official is responsible for tracking down. But suppose you don't have any idea about the requirements of the position? Suppose you're doing all the right things—avoiding fixation on the classifieds, isolating fast-growing employers, devoting a certain period of the day to cold calls to managers—and you *don't know* whether there's an opening that's right for you at a promising company? As luck would have it, you can still use a letter to your advantage. Consider the two samples that follow—each of which can, like the one you just saw, be adapted to those infrequent situations when you must pop a resume into the mail.

(Date)

Mr. John Miller
ABC Corporation
456 Main Street
Mytown, State 00000

Dear Mr. Miller:

According to *Business Week*, the American widget industry is poised for "significant expansion into Eastern European and South American medical equipment markets" within the next two years (*Business Week*, January 16, 1998, page 123). I applaud the groundbreaking work your firm is doing to expand into these new markets—and would love to be able to help contribute to your firm's steady growth. I gather from the *Business Week* article that your company is among those attempting to increase business significantly in these areas of the world. That being the case, you're likely to need help managing increased levels of inventory. I offer you:

>   Five years of superior high-efficiency performance in a widget inventory management environment

>   Superior computer skills and deep knowledge of both WidgetManager and Lotus 1-2-3

>   A team-first attitude and the ability to work both independently and as part of a workgroup

I will be in your area next week. I would like to visit with you so we can discuss how we might be able to work together to increase efficiency and reduce inventory management costs at your company.

Sincerely,

Jane Smith
123 Main Street
Mytown, State 00000
(555) 555-5555

P.S. I will plan on calling you at 9:00 A.M. on Tuesday, July 16th. If this is not a convenient time, please tell Robin a better time for me to call.

My experience has shown me that the postscript is the very best place to serve notice of what you plan to do next. The more you're able to customize the postscript—by, for instance, making reference to a secretary or assistant—the better off you'll be. And if you *reach* that secretary or assistant, don't get haughty or start ordering him or her around. Treat this person *exactly* as though he or she were the big boss.

Here's another example of an eye-catching cover letter that paves the way for a personal phone call. This one does the trick by highlighting a single example of superior performance that leaves the reader wanting to know more.

(Date)

Mr. John Miller
ABC Corporation
456 Main Street
Mytown, State 00000

Dear Mr. Miller:

I was named Inventory Manager of the Year at my company's national awards dinner last year because I reduced stockouts by 64% after only six months on the job. I'm a computer-savvy, goal-oriented team player who follows the widget industry closely. The January 16 issue of *Business Week* leads me to believe that expansion is in your company's future—and that you'll soon be in need of a qualified inventory specialist like me.

Let's meet to discuss the possibilities!

Sincerely,

Jane Smith
123 Main Street
Mytown, State 00000
(555) 555-5555

P.S. I plan to call you at 9:00 A.M. on Tuesday, July 16th. If this is not a convenient time, please tell Robin a better time for me to call.

As you've probably gathered, I'm a big believer in the less-is-more principle when it comes to job search letters. (I think the same basic principle applies to resumes, by the way; I've met too many hiring officials who hate reading multipage resumes to feel otherwise.) The aim, after all, is not to drown the (probably overloaded) reader in new facts, but to elicit that simple "WOW" reaction that leads naturally to the question, "When can you come by for an interview?" I've talked to plenty of hiring officials who felt overwhelmed by a resume that left little to the imagination … and, often, little to discuss with the applicant.

Here's one more effective employment letter that you may wish to use as a model, one that's based on a previous phone conversation between you and your contact. Note how it takes the bull by the horns, that is, takes responsibility for a dramatic "next step," and how it employs effective appeals based on points raised during your call.

(Date)

Mr. John Miller
ABC Corporation
456 Main Street
Mytown, USA 00000

Dear Mr. Miller:

It was great to talk to you recently concerning employment opportunities at ABC. I was particularly intrigued by what you had to say about the new widget outsourcing program, which I understand needs to be up and running very soon. With your permission, I'd like to put together an outline of an agreement that would allow me to help ABC develop a detailed plan of attack for your project on an "independent contractor" basis—including recommending vendors and developing training materials for the new software you'd need.

I'll plan on faxing my outline of how we might be able to work together to your attention this coming Friday, and I'll follow up by phone the following Monday.

Thanks for taking time to speak with me!

Sincerely,

Jane Smith
123 Main Street
Mytown, State 00000
(555) 555-5555

P.S. I plan to call you at 9:00 A.M. on Monday, July 15th. If this is not a convenient time, please tell Robin a better time for me to call.

Talk about creative pestering! The foregoing letter provides an excellent example of exactly what such "pestering" looks like when it's committed to paper. Did your contact volunteer anything about your working as an independent contractor for ABC? No—but there's certainly no reason not to bring the subject up yourself, especially if you've got some insight about where the company is going in the near future. Did your contact say anything about talking to you on Monday morning about your outline? No,—but simply faxing the material would probably lead to a long silence. What's the harm in following up persistently and politely?

Now it's time to take a look at the stars of our show— the model documents that will help you craft your own WOW resume! As you make your way through the main section of the book, remember that you're going to be talking to more than one potential employer over the course of your job search. That means you'll need more than one resume. Don't wed yourself to one single model from the examples that follow. Pick the format that provides the best "fit" with your situation and customize it to the needs and interests of the person and organization you're targeting.

4

Don't Send It Off Yet!

Double Check Everything

Chi Wen Tze always thought three times before acting. Twice would have been enough.

CONFUCIUS

No matter how excited you are about the opportunity you're pursuing, don't consider your resume and cover letter complete until you've consulted the following checklists!

There are plenty of resume horror stories making the rounds. I've heard tell of resume writers who committed grievous spelling errors in the very lines in which they boasted about their attention to detail; resume writers who focused on catastrophes at work that they vowed not to repeat, and resume writers who let ludicrously inappropriate word choices torpedo their chances for getting a good job. Don't let that happen to you! Follow these Commandments for Perfect Letters and Commandments for Perfect Resumes.

TEN COMMANDMENTS FOR PERFECT COVER LETTERS

Customize Your Document to Your Intended Audience.

Focus Your Remarks within a Few Concise Paragraphs, and Don't Exceed a Single Page.

Read Your Letter Carefully and, if Possible, Subject It to a Computerized Spell Check.

Then, in Addition to Your Computerized Spell Check, Enlist a Trusted, Literate Friend to Review Your Text for Spelling or Style Errors.

Never Bring Up Salary Unless Instructed by Your Contact to Do So, in Which Case Speak of Broadly Scaled Salary Ranges.

Never Focus on a Negative Element of Your Background.

Use the Word "I" with Restraint.

Include Full Contact Information in Your Letter.

Close Your Letter with a Promise of, or a Request for, Future Action.

Always Tell the Truth.

TEN COMMANDMENTS FOR PERFECT RESUMES

Customize Your Document to Your Intended Audience.

Do Not Box.

Read Your Resume Carefully and, if Possible, Subject It to a Computerized Spell Check.

Then, in Addition to Your Computerized Spell Check, Enlist a Trusted, Literate Friend to Review Your Text for Spelling or Style Errors.

Include Facts That Buttress Your Cause, and Only Facts That Buttress Your Cause, Never Confusing Your Resume with a Confessional Document.

Display Energy, Creativity, and Personality without Exceeding the Bounds of Good Taste and Professionalism.

Break Your Points Up into Readable Chunks.

Eliminate Fluff and Trivia That Does Not Supports Your Cause.

Include Full Contact Information in Your Resume.

Always Tell the Truth.

Review these lists, check them twice, bear them in mind as you compose your written appeals—and your campaign to land the health care job you deserve will have been well and truly launched.

Good luck!

5
The Resumes

Powerful accomplishments under "Performance Highlights"
spotlight this applicant's strong management skills.

JOHN SMITH   **45 Evansdale Drive, Anytown, State 00000 (555) 555-5555**

OBJECTIVE   A position in Nursing Administration where my experience, education, and personal abilities can be utilized to improve patient care and facility operations.

EXPERIENCE   10/61–Present   SCRANTON HOSPITAL CENTER, Pennsylvania
                      2/81–Present   ASSISTANT DIRECTOR OF NURSING, New York

Assignments have included: General Medicine, Drug and Alcohol Detoxification Medicine, R.S.C.U., M.I.C.U., and R.I.C.U.
Responsibilities include: coordinating staff of 9–30 employees, including five supervisors. Personnel Management: interviewing, hiring, training, scheduling, and evaluating personnel, and engaging in labor relations activities. Planning, implementing and directing programs.

Performance highlights:

Responsible for structuring, implementing and administering an inpatient alcohol detoxification unit.
Implemented alternate work scheduling to relieve staffing problems.
Created pilot program in Primary Nursing.
Implemented Clinical Instructor program for extended orientation, providing annual employee skills assessments.
Implemented interdisciplinary meetings on a monthly basis.
Implemented quality assurance program for Department of Medical Nursing.

Hospital-wide Committees:	Pharmacy and Therapeutics	Cancer
	Discharge Planning Problems	Risk Management
	Product Evaluation	

Nursing Committees:	Quality Assurance	Documentation
	Co-Chairperson, Policy and Procedures Committee	

5/79–2/81: SUPERVISOR OF NURSES, Medical Department
7/79–9/80:NURSE COORDINATOR, Interdisciplinary Hospice Team
7/77–5/79: NURSE CLINICIAN, GYN, GU, ENT, MEDICINE
9/76–7/77: CLASSROOM INSTRUCTOR, School of Nursing, Medical-Surgical Nursing
9/70–9/76: CLINICAL INSTRUCTOR, School of Nursing

Areas of instruction included:	Orthopedics	Pediatric Clinic
	Emergency Room	Medicine and Surgery

2/65–9/70: SUPERVISOR OF NURSES, Emergency Room/Nursing Office
3/63–2/65: HEAD NURSE, Medicine and Neurosurgery
10/61–3/63: STAFF NURSE, Medicine

EDUCATION   TEACHERS COLLEGE, PHILADELPHIA UNIVERSITY, Philadelphia, Pennsylvania
                      10/77: MASTER OF ARTS DEGREE, Teaching of Nursing

                      CRATEAL COLLEGE OF THE CITY UNIVERSITY OF HARRISBURG, Harrisburg, Pennsylvania
                      1/68: BACHELOR OF SCIENCE DEGREE, Nursing

                      SCRANTON HOSPITAL CENTER SCHOOL OF NURSING, Scranton, Pennsylvania
                      9/61: Diploma

PROFESSONAL   American Nurses Association

AFFILIATIONS   American Nurses Foundation Century Club
                      Pennsylvania State Nurses Association
                      Pennsylvania State Nurses Association, District 14
                      Crateal College Alumni Association
                      Nursing Education Alumni Association, Teachers College

REFERENCES
Available upon request.

An effective use of institution-specific targeting within the objective. Early positions not relevant to the field have been omitted for a concise, direct document.

JOHN JONES
45 Evansdale Drive, Anytown, State 00000 (555) 555-5555

OBJECTIVE
Seeking a challenging position as an Alcoholism Counselor at Greenway Medical Center.

QUALIFICATIONS
Have completed service in the field as a paid Alcoholism Counselor. Will sit for the CAC exam in October 1999.

WORK EXPERIENCE
ADULT SERVICES, Dubuque, Iowa   **1995–Present**
Alcoholism Counselor
Directly involved with counseling a client population; services center around alcoholism, its ramifications, the recovery process, etc. Work with a large number of mandated cases, engaging and empowering clients. Assess their needs and exercise prompt intervention techniques when necessary, directing clients to appropriate level of care and treatment, i.e., detox and medically managed inpatient facilities. Functioned as group leader: one early sobriety women's group and a DWI educational group. Maintain case documentation and review, accessing a full range of professional and community resources. Assist with transporting clients.

NEW ENERGY, St. Louis, Missouri   **1993–1995**
Alcoholism Counselor
Activities centered around phase one of a structured (14-month) rehabilitation program; specifically this involved Didactic Alcohol Education. Worked with a low socioeconomic population to inform them of the disease concept and the recovery tools. Worked with individuals and groups (15–30), developing psycho-socials and disclosing personal issues. Developed treatment plans. Worked as a team player. Facilitated groups: emotions/feelings, drinking and driving, relapse prevention, and aftercare groups. Interfaced with social workers, parole officers, CWAs, clinical supervisor, and confidential AIDS-related clients. Attended graduation ceremonies for clients who completed program.

TRANSFER INTERNATIONAL, Boston, Massachusetts   **1990–1993**
Administrator Assistant
Administrative responsibilities for this import/export company: updating calendar for several company principals, coordinating communications between support staff and supervisors, routinely preparing conference room for meetings. Kept accurate records, answered three phone lines.

VOLUNTEER WORK
Tutor, P.S. 201, Flushing, NY (1990–1991)
Pediatric Ward Volunteer, Boston General Hospital, Boston, Massachusetts (1990)

SPECIAL TRAINING/EDUCATION
BOSTON UNIVERSITY CONTINUING EDUCATION PROGRAM
Alcoholism
Counseling Training and Education (specific and relevant hours) Completed all course work in September 1995.

NEW HAVEN COMMUNITY COLLEGE, New Haven, Connecticut
Major: Liberal Arts/Social Science, 1983–1985

Reference Enclosed

Note the powerful use of an endorsement at the head of the resume.

MARY SMITH
45 Evansdale Drive,
Anytown, State 00000
(555) 555-5555

"Consistently accurate, dependable, and detail-oriented."—Faculty review, December 1997

EDUCATION

OHIO STATE UNIVERSITY, Columbus, Ohio
Master of Science, 1994
Major: Crop Sciences   G.P.A.: 3.88

BANGALORE AGRICULTURAL UNIVERSITY, Bangalore, India
Bachelor of Science, 1984
Course work included: Biochemistry, Organic and Inorganic Chemistry, Agricultural Microbiology, Plant Physiology, Human Nutrition
Merit Awards: 1981, 1982, 1983, 1984

PROFESSIONAL DEVELOPMENT

OHIO STATE UNIVERSITY, Columbus, Ohio 1991–present
Research Assistant
Participated in various research projects and experiments conducted by a team of faculty (Ph.D. and Masters degrees) and graduate students. These involved five separate projects ranging in scope of time (three months, four months, etc.); some results were published. The project involved working with laboratory models of cotton, soybeans, and other plant life and comparing patterns with those grown in the field. More specifically, this involved lab analysis of nitrogen content of different plant pans (Regular Kjeldahl Method), soluble protein (Bio-Rad Protein Assay), and chlorophyll analysis (acetone yield-extracts).

Studied cotton photosynthetic efficiency and capacity under low-light conditions to make determinations regarding plant growth and ultimately to increase production in the field. Examined the influence of photo period and temperature of soybean flower induction and flowering fruit development and cotton photosynthesis and plants grown under different sources: sink rations. Observed the characteristics of soybean flower development and collected data for cotton model validation and plant mapping. Utilized laboratory simulation models, conducted instrumental analysis with LICOR-6200, pressure chamber, etc.

MYSORE ACADEMY OF AGRICULTURAL SCIENCES, India 1984–1991
Research Assistant
As part of a research team, studied the effects of various nutrients on tiller development, vegetative growth, and grain yield; completed nutrient deficiency diagnosis in order to modify a technique used in rice culture for correcting wheat nutrient deficiencies. Studied methods to shorten intervals between rice and wheat stand establishment. Developed cultivation models of wheat for the hilly regions south of the Narmada River.

COMPUTERS
IBM PC, WordPerfect 5.1, SAS, Sigma Plot, REF11

Multiple professional objectives, carefully selected and held until near
the end of the resume, add interest and variety.

MARY SMITH
45 Evansdale Drive
Anytown, State 00000
(555) 555-5555

EDUCATION OVERVIEW
Portland Chiropractic College
Degree conferred: April 1982
Internship at Portland Community College Clinic

Activities:
Completed Portland Community College Lay Lecture Certificate Program; lay lectured in community; member of Portland Community College Nutrition Club; observer in office of Dr. Olson, Uniondale, New York; earned nearly 100% of tuition expenses through various full- and part-time employment.

Seminars Attended:

Peterson	Upper Cervical
Johnson-Pierce	Dynamic Essentials

Areas of Chiropractic Proficiency:

Full Spine Diversified Technic	Modalities
Upper Cervical Technic	Cox Analysis
Drop Pelvic/Cervical	Adjusting Children

UNDERGRADUATE EDUCATION
Oregon State College, 1973–1975; Salem State University at Salem, 1975–1978

PROFESSIONAL OBJECTIVES
Build and maintain a successful chiropractic practice through long-term associateship.
Cultivate community goodwill through civic involvement.
Enhance community perception of chiropractic by conducting lay lectures.

PERSONAL DATA
Born 9/5/55...Single...In Excellent Health.

REFERENCES
References will be furnished upon request.

An educational background with diverse elements
is highlighted to show breadth of experience.

MARY SMITH
45 Evansdale Drive
Anytown, State 00000
(555) 555-5555

Objective:	Seeking an associateship position as Doctor of Chiropractic
Education:	Bachelor of Science, Industrial Labor Relations, Harvard University Graduated May 1981 Dean's List, Total Grade Point Average: 3.04
	Lowell Community College, nondegree, 1992–93 Credit hours: 46 (Science prerequisites) Total Grade Point Average: 4.0 Phi Theta Kappa (National Honor Fraternity)
	Doctor of Chiropractic, Boston Chiropractic College January 1994–April 1997 Dean's List, Total Grade Point Average: 3.71 Phi Chi Omega Honor Society
Work Experience:	*President/Owner,* 1993–1994, Creatform Co., Inc., Brooklyn, N.Y.—a manufacturing firm with international markets, sold and presently operating under ownership by conglomerate
	Chiropractic Intern, Johnson Chiropractic Offices, Worcester, Massachusetts, 1997
Continuing Education:	Nimmo Technique (Myofascial Release), Dr. James Elliott December 1997, Lynn, Massachusetts
	Low Back Pain and Radiographic Interpretation, Harold Spence, D.C., D.A.C.B.R., and John Parker, D.C., D.A.C.B.R., March, 1997 Lowell State University, Massachusetts
	Radiological Studies, Barton Mackie, D.C., D.A.C.B.R., March 1996, April 1996, June 1996, Boston Chiropractic College
	Primary Characteristics and Sites of Bone Pathology, Martin Ebert, D.C., D.A.C.B,R., October 1987, Lynn, Massachusetts
Certification:	National Board of Chiropractic Examiners, Certificate number: 37409, includes Parts I, II, Physiotherapy, and Written Clinical Competency Examination (WCCE).
	Massachusetts State Licensure: presently awaiting results of State Board Examinations
References:	Harold B. Fine, D.C., D.A.B.C.O. 45 East 45th Street, #1C, Boston, MA
	Peter Barrow, D.C. 1653 Massachusetts Avenue, Cambridge, MA
	Additional references furnished upon request.

Note the targeted objective and the compelling use of an
(approved) testimonial near the beginning of the resume.

MARY SMITH
45 Evansdale Drive
Anytown, State 00000
(555) 555-5555

OBJECTIVE: To become Nursing Cluster Coordinator at Fisher Medical Center

EXPERIENCE:

3/94–12/97 CHICAGO HOSPITAL, ILLINOIS STATE MEDICAL CENTER, Chicago, Illinois

STAFF NURSE AND PRECEPTOR
- Semimodified primary nurse-oriented care.
- District Leader for shift. Praised by head nurse for "initiative, administrative ability, thoroughness, and tireless dedication to patients."

Intensive Care

CARDIOTHORACIC INTENSIVE CARE UNIT
- Decision-making responsibilities.
- Receive one to two patients nightly, primarily in cardiac arrest.

Aids Forum
Lecturer—Educational and support group for nurses and other hospital staff.

Clinical Highlights Series
Program instituted for the recruitment of nurses.

EDUCATION:

ILLINOIS STATE UNIVERSITY, Springfield, Illinois
Bachelor of Science in Nursing, 1983

CHAMPAIGN COMMUNITY COLLEGE, Champaign, Illinois
Associate of Science in Nursing, 1982
Member—Sigma Theta Tau (International Honor Society of Nursing)

Emphasis on "Special Training" helps this applicant stand out—as does the diversity of experience supported by the final entry detailing military experience.

MARY SMITH

45 Evansdale Drive
Anytown, State 00000
(555) 555-5555

DENTAL ASSISTANT

EDUCATION and SPECIAL TRAINING

DU BOIS UNIVERSITY, Du Bois, Pennsylvania
Doctor of Dental Science, 1994

Courses and lab work:

- Surgery
- Periodontics
- Radiology
- Dental Materials Science
- Infectious Disease Control
- Ethical and Legal Aspects
- Gained practical experience while working in the dental clinic affiliated with the school.

Responsibilities included working alongside dentists, assisting with maxilla facial surgery and other problems of the teeth and gums. Helped to prepare patients, and performed preliminary examinations of patients' mouths. Cleaned teeth, sterilized and disinfected equipment.

Currently preparing for the National Dental Boards, scheduled exam date, December 1995

FOREMAN DENTAL INSTITUTE, Jacksonville, Florida
Completed one-year of training as a Dental Technician, 1990.

- Training included all phases of building porcelain crowns and bridges.

EXPERIENCE

1995–Present   *HAROLD P. MARTIN,* Jacksonville, Florida
Assistant to Prosthodontic Specialist

Assist with all phases pertaining to crown and bridgework, implants, partial attachments, and acrylic work.

This is a state-of-the art office.

1982–1983   *SAMIA DENTAL LABORATORY,* Tampa, Florida
Dental Technician

Activities focused on all phases of acrylic work, setup of teeth, and waxing, including everything necessary to construct complete dentures. Responsible for making molds, preparing temporary pieces for crowns and bridges, and polishing finished products, as well as the repair of dentures.

MILITARY

1983–1988   *U.S. ARMY*
Stationed at Fort Bragg, Hawaii
E4 Specialist
Completed training in tactical communications. Cited three times for operational excellence.

Less is more! An admirably concise summing-up of an impressive career—where other job seekers might have used a multiple-page format to say half as much.

JOHN SMITH
45 Evansdale Drive
Anytown, State 00000
(555) 555-5555

PROFESSIONAL OVERVIEW:
A skilled dentist with experience in treating patients of all ages and special proficiency in the dental problems of the elderly.

1965–Present	MOBILE CARE, Sacramento, California
	Founder and Director—Dentistry for homebound patients since 1983.
1976–Present	CHEMICAL SEARCH CO., Fresno, California
	Consultant

HOSPITAL AFFILIATION:

1972–1981	SACRAMENTO COMMUNITY HOSPITAL, Sacramento, California
	Associate Attending

Director of Dentistry at the following Nursing Homes:

HOLLYDALE NURSING HOME, Modesto, California
MEADOWVIEW CARE CENTER, Sacramento, California
MARY BARTON HEALTH CARE CENTER, Roseville, California
VILLAGE VIEW, Modesto, California
MASON HEIGHTS, Sacramento, California
CLEARWATER NURSING HOME, Fresno, California
GLEN HAVEN NURSING HOME, Modesto, California
MARY'S REST HOME AND CARE CENTER, Madera, California
VISTA GARDEN HOME, Madera, California
SWEET ORCHARD HOME AND NURSING CENTER, Turlock, California

PROFESSIONAL ASSOCIATIONS:

Sacramento County Dental Society
Academy of General Dentistry
Academy of Geriatric Dentistry
Academy of Dentistry for the Handicapped

EDUCATION:

Fellow in the Academy of General Dentistry, 1975
UNIVERSITY OF CALIFORNIA LOS ANGELES—D.D.S., 1973
SAN FRANCISCO STATE UNIVERSITY—B.S., 1967

A concise, no-frills summary with relevant academic achievements
highlighted—and a compelling opening summary.

MARY SMITH
45 Evansdale Drive, Anytown, State 00000 (555) 555-5555

SUMMARY
An experienced, caring dentist who puts patients first.

EDUCATION
D.M.D. MADISON UNIVERSITY, SCHOOL OF DENTISTRY, 1984
    Madison, Wisconsin
    Honors: Selected as Associate Member of the Endodontology Society
STATE UNIVERSITY OF MICHIGAN AT GRAND RAPIDS, 1980
    Grand Rapids, Michigan
    B.S. in Biology
    Graduated *magna cum laude*
    B.A. in Studio Art, 1980

PROFESSIONAL EXPERIENCE

General Dentist, Private Practice   12/86–Present
    Lansing, Michigan
    Modalities:
- Molar Root Canal Therapy
- Cosmetic Dentistry [including porcelain laminate veneers and cosmetic bonding]

General Dentist, Beaver Dam Dental Group   10/85–12/86
    Madison, Wisconsin
    Actively involved in progressive practice utilizing a holistic approach to treatment
    Modalities:
- Cosmetic Dentistry
- Nutritional Counseling
- Oral Cancer Screening
- Periodontics
- Prostodontics
- Analgesia

General Dentist, Madison Dental Clinic   7/84–9/85
    Madison, Wisconsin
    Modalities:
- Oral Surgery
- Endodontics
- Prosthodontics
- Periodontics

Pediatric Dentistry, Saint Clair's Hospital   9/83–1/84
    Madison, Wisconsin
    Intensive internship program revolving around periodontia and the use of nitrous oxide.

General Dentist, Atwater Hospital   2/84
    Warren, Pennsylvania

SEMINARS
Registered for L.D. Continuum I, Harris Institute
- American Sign Language, New York Society for the Deaf, Lansing, Michigan
- Periodontics Seminar
- Occlusion Seminar, First District Dental Society

ASSOCIATIONS
A.D.A,, Madison Study Group Associate Member of Oral Surgery, Associate Member of Endodontic Society, Alpha
Omega, Lansing Dental Society, American Society of Dentistry for Children.

A superior summary of relevant professional experience from a recent graduate.

MARY SMITH
45 Evansdale Drive, Anytown, State 00000 (555) 555-5555

OBJECTIVE   To deliver comprehensive dental care in a high-quality setting.

LICENSE   Massachusetts State, Northeast Regional Boards

POSTGRADUATE TRAINING
> 7/95–6/96 General Practice Residency (1 year), Lowell Memorial Medical Center, Lowell, Massachusetts

EDUCATION
ADAMS FULLER UNIVERSITY, Springfield, Massachusetts, School of Dentistry
> 1995 Doctor of Dental Medicine
> *Honors:*
> American Society of Dentistry for Children, Certificate of Merit
> Student Teaching Fellowship Award, Dept. of Pediatric Dentistry
> Letter of Commendation for Academic Achievement
> *Activities:*
> 1991–1992 Class Representative, Dept. of Anatomy and Histology
> 1992–1993 Class Secretary, Final Examination Committee
> 1993–1994 Class Secretary; Class Representative, Dept. of Pharmacology, Final Examination Committee, Admissions Committee Tour Guide
> 1994–1995 Class Secretary; Yearbook Committee; Senior Student Teaching Fellowship, Dept. of Pediatrics; Senior Student elected to School of Dentistry Admissions Committee

STATE UNIVERSITY OF MASSACHUSETTS, WORCESTER, Worcester, Massachusetts
> 1990 Bachelor of Arts Degree in Biology
> *Honors:*
> Dean's List for four years.

PROFESSIONAL EXPERIENCE
LYNN DEVELOPMENTAL CENTER, Lynn, Massachusetts
CONCORD PSYCHIATRIC HOSPITAL, Concord, New Hampshire
> Summer, 1994 Dental Extern. Responsible for completing a four-week dental externship program in these two medical facilities.
> Provided a full range of dental services to both children and adults.
> Evaluated patients, directed the management and treatment of medically compromised and handicapped individuals.
> Interfaced effectively with Medical Directors concerning the evaluation, treatment, and progress of patients.

MARY SMITH
45 Evansdale Drive
Anytown, State 00000
(555) 555-5555

OBJECTIVE
Seeking a challenging full-time position, working for either a single practitioner or in a clinic setting.

PROFILE
Successful experience working for various dental practices in the metropolitan area including an expanding dental clinic...

Organized professional, with demonstrated ability to assist alongside dentists, thereby increasing productivity...

Able to coordinate multiple projects and work well with individuals on all levels...

A people person, sensitive and perceptive, with extensive, customer/client contact...

Demonstrated ability to develop and maintain sound relationships with customers, anticipating their needs.

SUMMARY OF QUALIFICATIONS
Able to assist with a variety of dental procedures to treat all types of problems of the teeth and mouth

Perform intraoral and extraoral examinations.

Help out with all operative procedures: the treatment of cavities, broken or chipped teeth, teething gum problems and gingivitis, installing crowns, braces, retainers, dentures, and other artificial teeth.

Assist with surgical procedures.

Take dental radiographs (X-rays).

Prophylaxis procedures, i.e., periodontal scaling and root planing.

Apply fluoride and sealers to help retard cavities in youngsters.

Maintain and manage compliance with OSHA regulations.

Oral hygiene evaluation instruction and maintenance.

PROFESSIONAL DEVELOPMENT
JOANNA GRANT, DDS/PETER BARNETT, DDS, Salina, Kansas 1994–Present
Dental Hygienist, Pediatric Practice

HARRINGTON DENTAL CENTERS, Harrington, Kansas 1994–Present
Dental Hygienist

DAVID CARSON, DDS, Great Bend, Kansas 1990–Present
Dental Hygienist, Periodontal Practice

LOREESE DUTTON, DDS, Garden City, Kansas 1987–Present
Dental Hygienist/Dental Assistant
This practice has a large number of elderly and homebound or disabled patients, servicing eight nursing homes.

EDUCATION
SALINA TECHNICAL COLLEGE, Salina, Kansas
Associate's Degree in Applied Sciences—Dental Hygienist
Graduated in top 10% of the class

REFERENCES
Available upon request.

The crisp "Professional Overview" puts the rest of this concise,
impressive resume in perspective.

John Smith
45 Evansdale Drive
Anytown, State 00000
(555) 555-5555

PROFESSIONAL OVERVIEW

January 89 to Present	Acting Chairman, Department of Radiology Cincinnati Hospital
April 83 to January 89	Associate Director, Department of Radiology Cincinnati Hospital
July 73 to April 83	Fellow, Assistant and Associate Attending Chairman of Isotope Committee In charge of special procedures

EDUCATIONAL BACKGROUND

Graduate	University of Bern, Switzerland, School of Medicine M.D., 1966.
Postgraduate	Columbus Hospital Medical Center Intern, 1969–70
	State University of Ohio, Down State Medical Center Resident in Diagnostic Radiology, 1970–73

ACCREDITATION & LICENSES

Diplomate of American Board of Radiology, 1975

OHIO Medical License

ILLINOIS Medical License

OREGON Medical License

PROFESSIONAL SOCIETIES

Member of:

American College of Radiology

The Society of Nuclear Medicine

American Institute of Ultrasound in Medicine

The emphasis on bilingual skills at the end of the resume sends
an important "buy" signal for this position.

JOHN SMITH
45 Evansdale Drive
Anytown, State 00000
(555) 555-5555

OBJECTIVE: Training in an Emergency Medicine residency program, which offers the best possible academic and hands-on working environment.

EDUCATION:

9/91–Present	HOUSTON MEDICAL COLLEGE, Houston, Texas
1/89–12/90	TEXAS STATE UNIVERSITY, Houston School of Medicine (Basic Science studies)
2/87	DALLAS COMMUNITY COLLEGE, City University of New York Bachelor of Arts, Biology
6/81	DALLAS TECHNICAL HIGH SCHOOL, Dallas, Texas

CERTIFICATION:

NATIONAL BOARD OF MEDICAL EXAMINERS—Part I, June 1991

UNITED STATES MEDICAL LICENSING EXAMINATION—Step 2, March 1993

EXTRACURRICULAR ACTIVITIES:

Undergraduate: Science Organization of Minority Students, two-time biathlon participant

HEALTH-RELATED ACTIVITIES:

MEDICAL TECHNICIAN, TEXAS DIAGNOSTIC CENTER (1986–1989)
Worked closely with physicians and administrators in this HMO. My duties included performing electrocardiographs, tonometry exams, pulmonary function tests, audiology exams, vision tests, and phlebotomy.

PHLEBOTOMIST, SURRY MEDICAL LABORATORY, HOUSTON, TEXAS (1987)
Member of early morning teams sent out from the main lab in Houston to work at nursing homes throughout the Houston and Galveston area.

OUTSIDE INTERESTS:

Scuba Diving, Skiing, Basketball, Reading

LANGUAGES:

English and Spanish, written and spoken.

The placement of emergency-room experience in the bottom third
of the resume adds interest and impact.

MARY SMITH
45 Evansdale Drive
Anytown, State 00000
(555) 555-5555

OBJECTIVE   A position as a Gastroenterologist and Internist where my experience, educational background, and
professional skills can be utilized for effective patient care.

MEDICAL BACKGROUND:
Gastroenterotogy
Fellowship: Phoenix Hospital, Phoenix, Arizona   7/83–Present
Complete direct patient care activities; interfacing with up to 40 new patients per week.
Procedures utilized include endoscopy techniques (gastroscopy, colonoscopy, polpectomy, ERCP, lim-
ited biliary surgery) and biopsy techniques.
Clinical Preceptor for extern program; planning and implementation of medical student educational
program; instructor in physical diagnoses; delivering academic lectures on gastroenterology and internal medicine.

Clinical Medicine
Fellowship: Phoenix Hospital, Phoenix, Arizona   7/82–6/83
Coordinated all activities of house staff of approximately 30 physicians and medical personnel;
oversaw sign-in rounds.
Lecturer for house staff; training staff in diagnosis and institutional management techniques.
Lecturer in Internal Medicine for house staff.
Chief Resident in charge of Intensive Care Unit.
Clinical Preceptor to externs.

Internal Medicine
Residency: Phoenix Hospital, Phoenix, Arizona   1/79–6/82
Pediatrics, Internal Medicine, and Emergency Room

RELATED PROFESSIONAL EXPERIENCE:
Phoenix Hospital, Phoenix, Arizona   1979–Present
EMERGENCY ROOM PHYSICIAN
Accumulated 3000 hours of Emergency Room experience.
Type of care provided includes: acute trauma, pediatric, gynecological, and medical emergency care.

EDUCATION:
Medical School: University of Stuttgart, Stuttgart, Germany   9/72–6/78
6/78: DOCTOR OF MEDICINE AND SURGERY DEGREE
Undergraduate: Arizona State University, Phoenix, Arizona   9/68–6/72
6/72: BACHELOR OF SCIENCE DEGREE, Biology
Activities and Honors: 1970–1972: Elected member of Alpha Epsilon Delta (Biology Honor Society).
1970–1972: Elected member of Phi Sigma (Biology Research Society).
1971–1972: President, Phi Sigma

CERTIFICATION:
9/82: Diplomate, Internal Medicine
American College of Physicians
7/85: Board Eligible—Gastroenterology

LICENSE: Licensed in Arizona for the practice of Medicine and Surgery.

PROFESSIONAL AFFILIATIONS: Associate Member, American College of Physicians.

REFERENCES: Available upon request.

A powerful and appropriately detailed professional profile pulls the reader
into this resume and replaces the common "objective" heading.

MARY SMITH
45 Evansdale Drive, Anytown, State 00000 (555) 555-5555

PROFESSIONAL PROFILE

I am a well-trained, highly organized individual with the ability to grasp new and complex situations, providing timely responses...Capable of developing an excellent working rapport with individuals of diverse backgrounds...Superior administrative and management skills...Extensive staff development and training background...I believe that the consistent, efficient manner in which I accept responsibilities, pursue assignments, and achieve all objectives will make me an asset to your organization.

EXPERIENCE

6/73–Present   Iowa State University Hospital, Council Bluffs, Iowa
11/79–Present: HEAD NURSE, MEDICAL I.C.U.

Responsibilities include:

Directly supervising activities of 35 employees; interviewing, hiring, orienting, training, scheduling, and evaluating personnel; conducting regularly scheduled staff meetings; interpreting policies and procedures for staff members; counseling personnel; ensuring staff development by initiating patient care conferences and assigning personnel to continuing education programs; terminating when necessary.

Ensuring quality care is administered in accordance with hospital standards; maintaining staffing levels; preparing monthly reports; participating on assigned committees.

Attending administrative meetings; initiating policies and programs; facilitating implementation of policy and program changes.

Maintaining awareness of inventory levels, ensuring the availability of adequate supplies and equipment.

Extensive interfacing with patients and professional staff; acting as liaison among patient, family physician, and hospital; providing continuity of care, acting as liaison between physician and health care team; making daily rounds; assisting staff with assessments of patients' needs and developing care plans.

Participating in nursing care as necessary; assisting in emergency situations.

2/77–11/79:   ASSISTANT HEAD NURSE, C.C.U.

Responsibilities included:

Assisting the head nurse in planning, organizing, directing, and supervising patient care in accordance with regulations and procedures of the institution; also overseeing the performance of nursing personnel in the unit in the absence of the Head Nurse.

6/73–2/77:   STAFF NURSE

EDUCATION

Des Moines Community College of the City University of Des Moines
1981: Courses toward Bachelor of Science Degree, Nursing
1973: Associate of Applied Sciences, Nursing

PROFESSIONAL DEVELOPMENT

DEPARTMENT OF HEALTH 1971–Present
Martin Case Child Health Clinic, Minneapolis, Minnesota

NURSE IN CHARGE (1982–Present)

Responsible for the overall management and administration of the clinic facility. Oversee and monitor policy standards, appointments, staffing, patient care, and records. Coordinate new programs (Primary Care Team Approach, Asthma Home and Developmental Screening), triages, refers and follow-up; counseling (genetic and HIV); administer immunization; visit homes; do nurse screenings and conferencing. Health teaching includes Asthma Support Group for parents and guardians, orientation and training of new nurses and other health professionals assigned to the clinic. Acted as Assistant Clinics Director when the region had none. Submitted accurate statistics on time.

STAFF NURSE (1971–1982)

Performed as Acting Nurse in Charge when necessary. Participated voluntarily in Triage Pilot Study for Pediatric Clinic. Did nurse conferences, home visits, referrals and follow-ups for the schools, Chest Clinics, S.T.D. Clinic, Child Health and Pediatric Clinics. On home visits did newborn inspections and postpartum exams. In the schools gave immunizations, teacher-nurse conferences, and health teaching. Coordinated and opened first Adolescent Clinic in Marshall Health Center.

HISTOLOGY TECHNICIAN

A detailed "Experience" section sets out appropriate technical requirements and accomplishments—without overwhelming the reader with supporting information.

JOHN SMITH
45 Evansdale Drive, Anytown, State 00000 (555) 555-5555

OBJECTIVE A full-time position as an Histology Technician, where my 27 years of professional experience, my educational background, and capacity for effective patient care can be utilized to our mutual benefit.

EXPERIENCE

7/83–Present   AMERICAN WELLNESS LABORATORIES, Los Angeles, California
HISTOLOGY (WORKING) SUPERVISOR

Monitoring day-to-day operations of high-volume histology laboratory.

Supervising up to eight employees; routinely overseeing and performing embedding, cutting, staining and cover-slipping of specimens.

Scheduling subordinates, full and part time.

Full knowledge of gross specimens of POCs (products of conceptions), skin, GYN, and gastrointestinal biopsies, familiar with bone and nail specimen handling.

Responsible for proper record keeping and compilation of monthly and yearly statistics.

In charge of ordering supplies for the department.

Performing various histochemical stains routinely as requested, including:

Grocott's Silver Methenamine (GSM), Acid Fast (AFB), IRON, Giemsa (MAY-Grunwald); Reticulum; Van Gieson; Warthin Starry stain for Donovan Bodies, Mast Cell Stain. Brown-Brenn for Bacteria; Amoeba stain; Congo Red for Amyloid, Crystal Violet for Amyloid; Fontana-Masson for Melanin; Mayer's Muci-carmine; Alcian Blue for Acid Mucosaccharides; Masson's Trichrome Stain.

Beginning to get involved in immunoperoxidase staining.

Attended wet workshops for immunoperoxidase staining conducted by the DACO Corporation and by Lipshaw Corp.

Engaged in quality control on a daily basis.

Daily checking of surgical slides prior to receipt by the pathologist for quality assurance.

Numerous body fluid preparation and staining.

Fully responsible and in charge of inspections for the Histology Department by various agencies—city, state, federal, and others.

Equipment utilized includes:

Autotechnicon Duo
Technicon's Decathlon Tissue Processing System
Full knowledge of V.I.P. (Vacuum Infiltrating Processor)
Utilizing the Fisher Auto-Stainer for routine H.E. staining.

6/70–7/83   RADIENT BIOMEDICAL INC. (formerly Path-TEK Medical Laboratories, Inc.)
HISTOLOGY TECHNICIAN

Supervising activities in the Histology Department, including:

Embedding, cutting, staining of specimens.
Staining large volume of Pap smears.
Frequent performance of special staining activities.
Engaging in routine and experimental tissue preparation.
Grossing POCs skin bone and nail Specimen

The emphasis on relevant educational achievements makes a compelling case for entry to a senior administrative position.

JOHN SMITH 45 Evansdale Drive Anytown, State 00000 (555) 555-5555

PROFESSIONAL OBJECTIVE

A responsible and challenging career opportunity where my professional background, strong organizational and personal skills, and my commitment to excellence will be of value and allow for professional growth . . . and my higher education in Health Care Administration will be fully utilized in a reputable health care organization/hospital known for its outstanding quality of management and devotion to providing patient care.

EDUCATIONAL BACKGROUND

1987 WASHINGTON STATE UNIVERSITY, Spokane Campus, Brookville, Washington, USA
Master of Public Administration in Health Care Administration

Coursework included Hospital Organization . . . Public Health and Regulations . . . Legal Aspects in Health Care Administration... Mental Health Administration... Long-Term Care Administration.

Authored an extensive thesis focusing on Voluntary and Municipal Hospital Pharmacies and their utilization of Pharmacists, with an analysis of selected activities.

1972 UNIVERSITY OF ALBERTA, Alberta, Canada
Bachelor of Pharmacy

LICENSURE

1978 Registered Pharmacist (New York State)

CIVIL SERVICE EXAMINATION

SEATTLE HEALTH & HOSPITALS CORPORATION

One of 198 candidates who filed and took the November 1983 Technical-Oral Exam for Senior Associate Pharmacist

Received the 6th highest grade within the Drug Information Category . . . Received the 8th highest score in the Outpatient/Inpatient Drug Dispensing Category.

Qualified for Senior Associate Pharmacist Levels A, B, and C (equivalent to Senior Pharmacist, Supervising Pharmacist, and Principal Pharmacist, respectively).

AFFILIATIONS

1975–AMERICAN SOCIETY OF HEALTH-SYSTEM PHARMACISTS
Present Member

1987–WASHINGTON STATE COUNCIL OF HEALTH-SYSTEM PHARMACISTS
Present Member

1990–WASHINGTON STATE SOCIETY OF HOSPITAL PHARMACISTS
Present Member

PROFESSIONAL BACKGROUND

1979–ALBERTA COUNTY HOSPITAL CENTER, Alberta, Canada
Present Senior Associate Pharmacist Level C—Principal Pharmacist (1989–present)

Responsible for directing and supervising the busy outpatient pharmacy operation for one of the largest acute care hospitals in the USA with over 1,200 beds. This is the largest municipal hospital in the major metropolitan area with a total of 140 outpatient clinics. Additionally, it is a major teaching hospital and is affiliated with the College of Medicine and School of Graduate Studies of the State University of Washington, Health Science Center at Brooklyn, Seattle.

(June 1995–present)

Supervise Pharmacists, Pharmacy Interns, and Office Aides, providing effective delegation of responsibility... Improved staff efficiency, morale, and overall service levels, which in turn has a direct positive impact on Pharmacy Department and entire hospital operations.

Duties also include supervising the dissemination of drug information to hospital staff and patients... Responsible for the requisitioning and receipt of drugs and supplies.

Experience of computerized hospital pharmacy practice including decentralized pharmacies, unit dose drug distribution system, preparing TPN, etc.

Additional responsibilities include maintaining accurate records of various supplies received, prescriptions filled, and drugs dispensed.

Coordinate and cooperate with different departments of the hospital, discussing methods of improving the hospital operations... Interface successfully with senior management.

Was responsible for directing and supervising the entire Pharmacy Department Operation in this hospital from 4:00 P.M. to midnight shift for over 15 years (December 1979–June 1995).

Senior Associate Pharmacist Level B—Supervising Pharmacist (1988)

Senior Associate Pharmacist Level A—Senior Pharmacist (1979–1988)

Pharmacist (1979)

PROFESSIONAL PROFILE

A highly organized and well-trained individual, with ability to develop excellent working rapport with people of various backgrounds... Excellent management and communication skills.

Able to grasp new and complex situations, providing timely responses... An adaptable individual with skills that are highly transferable… Works well under pressure.

The consistent manner in which responsibilities are accepted, as well as the way objectives and goals are pursued and accomplished, will make this individual a valuable asset.

References Furnished Upon Request

A powerful summary provides an excellent introduction to a detailed
discussion of experience. Note the effective use of action verbs
(guide, expand, recruit, review, create, maintain).

MARY SMITH
45 Evansdale Drive, Anytown, State 00000 (555) 555-5555

OBJECTIVE

To obtain a position as Hospital Director at Berwick Medical Center.

SUMMARY OF QUALIFICATIONS

Successfully guided areas of responsibility through accreditation procedures with various regulatory agencies... Objectively dealt with all medical and professional service departments... Updated and reviewed all division policies and procedures, making timely recommendations when appropriate... Oversaw recruitment and personnel supervision... Handled credentialing and dissemination of all relevant information to appropriate staff

PROFESSIONAL EXPERIENCE

DENVER HOSPITAL AND MEDICAL CENTER, Denver, Colorado, 1989–present
Present Associate Director/North Division (9/90–present)
Major activities center on planning, coordinating, implementing, and evaluating nursing care.

Administrative responsibilities:

Successfully established division as a multiservice sector with special emphasis on the development of the Ambulatory Surgery Unit.

Assisted extensively with expanding the Pulmonary Care Unit and Rehabilitation Medicine services.

Developed and implemented additional intrahospital transfer policies.

Introduced and established decisive management practices with the emphasis on fiscal constraint.

Responsible for developing annual capital budgets, including salaries and expenditures.

As part of day-to-day operations, routinely interfaced with all relevant departments.

Delegated nursing responsibilities to Nursing Supervisors.

Nursing responsibilities:

Ambitiously participate in designing challenging long- and short-range programs for the nursing service.

Collaborate in the annual progressive development of the organizational plan of nursing services, providing direction to supervisors as they develop organization unit design.

Actively recruit and select professional and nonprofessional personnel for positions within the department.

Expand the potential of the supervisory personnel in working with their respective clinical areas, in order to formulate innovative staffing patterns and to satisfy the goals of the nursing service in an expedient and efficient manner.

Comprehensively assist in the preparation of the annual nursing service budget, using established indicators to manage and monitor the budget on a monthly basis, resulting in recommendations for future budget formulation.

Capably create and maintain professional liaison with appropriate internal and external groups.

Assistant Director of Nursing for Medical Surgical Service/Dept. of Nursing (1989–1990)
Primary responsibilities centered on appraisal of existing objectives within the department, arranging, setting up, and coordinating new goals. Additionally charged with providing excellent patient care and promoting the best possible guest relations.

Nursing and Administrative responsibilities:

Ambitiously participated in designing short- and long-term goals for the Medical/Surgical Nursing Service.

Strategically collaborated with other leadership personnel in formulating, defining, and interpreting policies.

Industriously participated in the development of annual organizational programs and authorized work assignments.

Prepared budgets, providing adequate staffing, as well as necessary capital expenditures, always keeping in mind the assurance of the quality for care.

Recruited, interviewed, and selected candidates for employment; promoted, counseled, and handled disciplinary actions according to existing policy; and terminated when indicated.

Collaborated with In-Service Nursing Department for purposes of implementing continuing educational programs to meet department needs.

STANFORD MEDICAL PRACTICE STUDY, Palo Alto, California, 6/88–9/88
Consultant
Team Leader responsible for coordination of MRA in intensive analysis of physician malpractice and litigation problems.

SAN JOSE HOSPITAL CENTER, San Jose, California, 1981–Present
Administrative Supervisor (Tour III)
Supervisor of Nurses (Emergency Department)

SANTA ROSA HOSPITAL, Santa Rosa, California, 1974–1981
Assistant Head Nurse (Emergency Department)
Staff Nurse

EDUCATION AND CERTIFICATION

AMERICAN NURSES CREDENTIALING CENTER
Certification in Nursing Administration, January 1991

ST. JOHN'S UNIVERSITY, San Francisco, California
Master of Science in Education, 1985

DENVER STATE COLLEGE, Denver, Colorado
Bachelor of Science in Education, 1981

DENVER HOSPITAL SCHOOL OF NURSING, Denver, Colorado
Professional Nursing Program

ASSOCIATIONS

American Association for Counseling and Development; New York State Nurses Association; Emergency Nurses Association; American Nurses Association.

REFERENCES

Personal and professional references available upon request.

Note the emphasis on bilingual skills, which can be a major advantage in some situations.

JOHN SMITH
45 EVANSDALE DRIVE, ANYTOWN, STATE 00000 (555) 555-5555

OBJECTIVE
To enter into a group practice upon completion of residency in June 1998.

MEDICAL EDUCATION:
MADRID MEDICAL COLLEGE (University of Madrid, Spain) 1993

M.B., B.S. Degree

TOEFL EXAM: Score, 640; Percentile 97% 1993. Fluent in both English and Spanish.

FLEX EXAM: From Board of California, Score: FWA 81% 1993

E.C.F.M.G.: Standard Certificate #334-378-7 1991

Electives: Evaluation and Treatment of Anemia 1990
        Health & Nutrition of Infants

PREMEDICAL EDUCATION:
UNIVERSITY OF CASTILE, Castile, Spain 1983–1985
Class Standing: 100/600
Received Awards in sports activities.

MIDDLE COLLEGE, Castile, Spain 1983
Distinction Grades; English Award

EXPERIENCE:
Grace Medical Center, Raleigh, North Carolina 7/95–Present
Affiliate of Cornell University
Internal Medicine Resident possessing comprehensive experience as House Physician at St. Francis and St. John's Hospital of Raleigh. Work in various departments including gastroenterology, cardiology, and hematology. Administer critical care, emergency, and continuing care in outpatient clinic. Perform various procedures including Swan Ganz Catheterization. Attend CME lectures and work emergency room, and on-call rotations. Received superior evaluations.

Winston-Salem General Hospital, Winston, North Carolina 9/91–10/92
Externship (Dept. of Cardiology)

St. Francis Hospital, Raleigh, North Carolina 1/93–4/93
Attended lectures and conferences.

Columbia General Hospital, Columbia, South Carolina 9/92–10/93
Laboratory Assistant

Madrid, Spain 1/91–4/91
General Physician (Private Practice)

Mostoles General Hospital, Madrid, Spain 7/90–1/91
Internship (medical, surgical, gynecology, obstetrics)

INTERNIST (INTERNATIONAL BACKGROUND)

MARK LEE
45 Evansdale Drive
Anytown, State 00000
(555) 555-5555

OBJECTIVE: RESIDENCY PGY-3 (Internal Medicine) July 1, 1998

EDUCATIONAL BACKGROUND:

July 1989–Passed ECFMG Examination

1985–Secured the MBBS Degree of the University of Ayutthaya, Bangkok, Thailand at the end of successful completion of five years of intensive studies covering the following courses:

Anatomy, Physiology, Biochemistry, Biophysics, Pathology, Pharmacology, Forensic Medicine, Ophthalmology, Obstetrics, Gynecology, Medicine, and Surgery

1979–Successfully completed the two-year Premed program of the University of Ayutthaya, which covered Physics, Chemistry, and Biology

1975–Graduation from High School in Bangkok, Thailand

HANDS-ON EXPERIENCE:

July 1997–Present   PGY-2 Internal Medicine, Minneapolis General Hospital,
Minneapolis, MN

1996–1997   PGY-1 Internal Medicine, Minneapolis General Hospital,
Minneapolis, MN

1991–1996   Lab Technologist, St. Cloud Community Hospital,
St. Cloud, MN

1989–1992   Postgraduate Course in Medicine at Stanley H. Kaplan Institute,
New York.

1986–1988   General Practice, Chang-Mai Clinic
Nakhon, Thailand

1986–1985   Rotating Intern, Khon Kean Hospital
Nakhon, Thailand, covering the following areas:

Two months in Medicine (including Forensic Medicine); two months in Surgery (including Orthopedics and Medicine); two months in Gynecology, Obstetrics, and Opthalmology; three months in Preventive and Social Medicine, including residency in rural areas for Public Health work; three months as medical officer at District Hospital, Nakhon, Thailand.

HOBBIES:

Soccer, Yoga, Classical Music, Reading, and Swimming.

OTHER:

U.S. citizen; married, three children.

The decision to lead the resume with a test result is fully justified by the applicant's achievement on the test. The first line highlights information that shouldn't be "buried" in the body text.

MARY SMITH
45 Evansdale Drive, Anytown, State 00000 (555) 555-5555

EDUCATION

January 1991	American Board of Internal Medicine In-Training Examination—98th Percentile
June 1990	FLEX (Component-I and II) ID #: 610827010
July 1989	ECFMG (Component-I and II) ID #: 423-815-0
May 1988	Master's Degree in Medicine (M.SC), Component I FACULTY of MEDICINE, CAIRO UNIVERSITY, Cairo, Egypt
March 1987	Ministry of Health Medical License, Cairo, Egypt
November 1985	M.B., B.Ch. (Bachelor of Medicine and Bachelor of Surgery degrees) FACULTY of MEDICINE, BADEN UNIVERSITY, Baden, Germany

PROFESSIONAL EXPERIENCE

July 1990–Present	STATE UNIVERSITY OF CALIFORNIA AT SAN FRANCISCO SAN FRANCISCO COUNTY MEDICAL CENTER, DEPARTMENT OF MEDICINE Resident in Internal Medicine
August 1989–February 1990	STATE UNIVERSITY OF CALIFORNIA AT SAN FRANCISCO SAN FRANCISCO COUNTY MEDICAL CENTER, DEPARTMENT OF MEDICINE Visiting Physician
June 1988–December 1988	NATIONAL RESEARCH CENTER, Frankfurt, Germany Research Fellow
April 1987–May 1988	AIR FORCE HOSPITAL, Mannheim, Germany Compulsory Military Service—Medical Resident
March 1986–March 1987	BADEN UNIVERSITY HOSPITAL Rotating Internship

ACHIEVEMENTS AND HONORS

January 1991

- Received Special Recognition/Commendation. Based on the evaluations and my scholastic accomplishments, the Residency Evaluation Committee of the Department of Medicine has selected me as the Outstanding House Officer.
- Graduated in the top 15% of my medical school class.
- Scholarship was awarded to me throughout my medical school years for my high scholastic achievements.
- Chosen to represent Baden University in the Annual Youth Conference in W. Germany and in the Youth Exchange Program to England, France, Italy, Greece, and Switzerland (Summer 1983).

MEMBERSHIP/SOCIETIES

- American Medical Association
- San Francisco Academy of Science
- American Association for Advancement of Science
- American College of International Physicians
- American College of Physicians, "Associate"

REFERENCES

Available upon request.

Note the inventive and unusually direct "Proficiencies" section, a real eye-catcher.

JOHN SMITH
45 Evansdale Drive, Anytown, State 00000 (555) 555-5555

PROFESSIONAL TRAINING

1996–present	Internal Medicine SHREVEPORT HOSPITAL 50th & LaFontaine, Shreveport, Louisiana 11418
1990–1991	Registered Medical Practitioner SOLO PRACTICE, Bangkok, Thailand
1988–1989	Rotary Internship KINGS COLLEGE AND ASSOCIATED HOSPITALS Chon Buri, Thailand

MEDICAL EDUCATION

1983–1988	M.B.B.S. KINGS MEDICAL COLLEGE, Chon Buri, Thailand

PROFESSIONAL EXAMINATIONS

E.C.F.M.G., 1993
FLEX, 1998

BOARD STATUS

Board eligible June 1998—American College of Physicians

MEDICAL LICENSES

New York, 1999

PROFESSIONAL MEMBERSHIP

Associate American College of Physicians
American Medical Association

PROFICIENCIES

Central Venous Line Placement
Swan Ganz Catheter Placement
Arterial Line Placement
Temporary Pacemaker Placement
Thoracentesis
Paracentesis
Spinal Tap
Endotracheal Intubation

WORK EXPERIENCE

SHREVEPORT HOSPITAL, Shreveport, Louisiana
Emergency Room
1000 hours of moonlighting experience in Inner City Trauma Center.
Medical Clinics
400 hours clinic experience in subspecialty areas of Pulmonary Diseases, Diabetes, Nephrology, Neurology, Rheumatology, Cardiology, and General Medical Clinics. Intensive Care Unit, Cardiac Care Unit.

PERSONAL DATA   U.S. Citizen, married

REFERENCES   Available upon request.

The "Education" section, emphasized early in the resume, highlights a major asset for this candidate—a superior record of academic achievement.

MARY SMITH
45 Evansdale Drive, Anytown, State 00000 (555) 555-5555

OBJECTIVE

Seeking a position in Internal Medicine where I can effectively utilize my experience to contribute to operational efficiency.

EDUCATION

ELMIRA STATE MEDICAL INSTITUTE, Elmira, NY

General Medicine—graduated *cum laude,* June 1990

- Research: Studied thyroid cancer in the Aral Sea area
- Recipient of scholarship for high grades
- President of Student Council
- Ranked First in Medicine, fifth and sixth semester
- Head Prefect, 1986–1990
- First Class honors in Physiology and Microbiology, June 1986

CURRENT PROFESSIONAL EXPERIENCE

Externship:

May 1995–Present

SAN ANTONIO V.A. MEDICAL CENTER, San Antonio, Texas

Attend patients as part of intake, taking and recording medical history, physical examination, and treatment. Attend Grand Rounds and Noon Conferences.

February 1995–Present

GALVESTON HOSPITAL CENTER, Galveston, Texas

Assembly/Chart Completion Unit

Assist with the completion of patients' medical records; review and follow up with laboratory test results.

Internship:

June 1990–July 1991

HOUSTON CITY HOSPITAL, Houston, Texas

Activities focused on Internal Medicine and Outpatient Clinic.

LICENSE

United States Medical Licensing Examination

Completed Steps I & II for Foreign Medical Graduates, and Step III.

Licensed to practice Medicine in France, July 1991

HOUSTON MEDICAL COLLEGE, Houston, Texas

Registered Nurse—graduated *cum laude,* September 1984

VOLUNTEER WORK

January 1995–Present

HOUSTON GENERAL HOSPITAL, Houston, Texas

Assist emergency-care patients with initial physical examinations, including lab work, and aid with the treatment of acute patients under the supervision of attending physicians.

PERSONAL

U.S. Permanent Resident

The confident, customized objective clarifies everything for the prospective employer.

MARY SMITH
45 Evansdale Drive
Anytown, State 00000
(555) 555-5555

OBJECTIVE

To make an immediate positive contribution to Dynahealth in the capacity of Lab Technologist, starting in early 1999—thanks to my family's upcoming relocation to your area.

PROFESSIONAL EXPERIENCE

RICHMOND UNIVERSITY HOSPITAL, Richmond, Virginia 11/96–Present
LAB TECHNOLOGIST

Apply molecular techniques to research projects, with particular emphasis in molecular biology, recombinant DNA manipulations, nucleic acid chemistry, and immunohistochemical areas.
*Project: Detection of genetic changes in human tumors and inherited cancer syndromes by comparative analysis of high-molecular-weight restriction enzyme cleavage patterns.
*Project: Gene rearrangements and viral involvement in human cancers.

NORFOLK LABORATORY, Norfolk, Virginia 8/94–11/96
RESEARCH TECHNICIAN

Developed working knowledge of molecular genetics, recombinant DNA techniques, tissue culture, and electrophoresis. Responsible for independent research, organizing and interpreting data.
*Maintained cell lines and virus stocks, performed protein fractination, antibody purification, immunoaffinity chromatography, immunoprecipitations, SDS Page electrophoresis, Western and Southern blotting.

CHARLOTTESVILLE ANIMAL LEAGUE, Charlottesville, Virginia 9/94
VETERINARY TECHNICIAN

Performed surgical preparation procedures and administered injections; recorded procedures/results and monitored animals' progress.

RALEIGH UNIVERSITY BIOLOGY DEPARTMENT, Raleigh, North Carolina 9/93–12/93
LABORATORY ASSISTANT 9/92–5/93

Lectured for General Biology class and organized experiments; administered and graded quizzes, corrected laboratory reports, and tutored students.

EDUCATIONAL BACKGROUND

RALEIGH UNIVERSITY, Raleigh, North Carolina
B.A. in Biology/Psychology 1994

Awards/Activities: Raleigh University Academic Scholarships (four years); Research Assistant (1993) and Behavioral Research Project (1991), Psychology Department; Research Assistant, Barrons Institute of Oceanography (1994); NASDS Certified Scuba Diver; Participate in Alumni Admissions Interview Program and College Fair Night, recruiting students.

PROFESSIONAL AFFILIATIONS

American Association for the Advancement of Science, American Association of Zoological Parks and Aquariums, Norfolk Zoological Society.

REFERENCES

Available promptly upon request.

A superior experience summary leads to a knockout "highlight film"
emphasizing relevant professional experience.

JOHN JONES
45 Evansdale Drive
San Francisco, CA 00000
(555) 555-5555

Seven years' experience . . .
. . . in operations management in the managed care industry
Three years' experience . . .
. . . in operations, budgeting, and finance in managed care environments.
Advanced degree . . .
. . . M.A. from Briarcliff University (1988) with concentrations in Healthcare and Business Administration

Professional Highlights

Senior Division Manager, ABC Health Plans. Reported directly to Regional Vice President, providing advice and research assistance on a wide variety of system and policy issues within the Pacific Northwest division. Assisted in acquisition of Yolliview Healthcare Associates. Managed, analyzed, and revised resource allocation and budget figures, resulting in **significantly reduced overlap and increased efficiency** following Yolliview acquisition. *(1993–1995)*

Service Center Manager, ABC Health Plans. Oversaw Northern California HMO Service Center, with broad-ranging responsibilities that included billing, enrollment, member services, and workmen's compensation. **Reduced operating expenses by 14 percent and improved cash flow** by means of new, more aggressive collections system. Revised policies and procedures throughout the Center, resulting in a **22 percent increase in operational effectiveness** as measured by standard company guidelines. *(1989–1993)*

Personnel Specialist, ABC Health Plans. Screened resumes, scheduled interviews, and updated job descriptions reflecting current ABC openings. Praised as **"versatile, organized, and highly efficient"** in 1988 salary review. *(1988–1989)*

Education

M.A., Briarcliff University, 1988. (See above.)

B.A, Weston College, 1986. Concentrations in Politics and Social Science. Maintained **3.8 grade point average; in addition, secured all tuition funds through personal savings and nighttime/weekend work secured through a local temporary agency.**

The opening educational summary demonstrates a commitment to continuing development.

JOHN SMITH
45 Evansdale Drive, Anytown, State 00000 (555) 555-5555

Passed the 1992 Certifying Examination in Internal Medicine on the first attempt since completing residency 15 years ago. Will take the April 12, 1997 examination to obtain a Certificate of Added Qualification in Geriatrics.

MEDICAL BACKGROUND

Professional Experience:

1993–Present Medical Director at Rene Vargas Institute, a 400-bed teaching nursing home affiliated with Phoenix York Medical College. Assistant Professor of Medicine, Phoenix Medical College.

1991–1993 Primary Care Physician at Native American Home & Hospital for the Aged, a teaching nursing home for the Phoenix Department of Geriatrics.

1980–1991 Internist and Pulmonary Specialist on the staff of New Orleans General Hospital. On the attending staff of several nursing homes.

Served in the following capacities:

Private Practice

    Physician Advisor with New Orleans General Hospital, responsible for utilization review from 1987–1988. Worksite Hypertension Control Program—Collaborative effort between Shreveport Medical College and various labor unions from 1980–1987.

Attending Medicine & Pulmonary:

JEFFERSON HOSPITAL, New Orleans, Louisiana

1978–1979 Charged with overseeing the activities of residents and interns.

Internal Medicine Residency & Pulmonary Fellowship:

1975–1978 ST. MARY'S MEDICAL CENTER/LOUISIANA COLLEGE OF MEDICINE
Designed and developed a research protocol correlating HLA types with asthmatic families, using exercise-induced bronchiospasm as the marker of disease.
Spent one month each at Memorial Bryan-Sartand and Cortland Hospitals.
Presentation: A Review of 23 Cases of Sarcoidosis, Louisiana Thoracic Society.

Internship:

1974–1975 CONNECTICUT MEDICAL COLLEGE, METROPOLITAN HOSPITAL CENTER, Hartford, Connecticut
Straight Medical Internship

EDUCATION

1972–1974 STATE UNIVERSITY OF CONNECTICUT, DOWNSTATE MEDICAL CENTER
Doctor of Medicine

1970–1972 BOSTON COLLEGE MEDICAL SCHOOL, Boston, Massachusetts
Master of Medical Science

1965–1970 HARTFORD COMMUNITY COLLEGE (Undergraduate)
Bachelor of Arts Degree—Chemistry

Activities and Honors:

    Graduated *cum laude,* 1970
    Graduated with Honors in Chemistry, 1970
    Chemistry Department Service Award, 1970
    Recipient of Regents Scholarship

LICENSE
Licensed to practice medicine in Connecticut, Louisiana, and Arizona

"Relocation? No problem." This resume sends that message
loud and clear in the opening paragraph.

JOHN SMITH
45 Evansdale Drive
Anytown, State 00000
(555) 555-5555

GEOGRAPHICAL REQUIREMENTS
OPEN for relocation

POSITION OBJECTIVE
Materials Manager in the Medical Industry

GENERAL SUMMARY
BS in Psychology, graduate study in Business Management and DP, 20 years' experience with emphasis on MATERIALS MANAGEMENT, HOSPITAL LOGISTICS SUPPORT, Budget Administration/Review, Staff Training/Supervision, Medical Assistance Programs, OPERATIONAL AUDITS, Cost Control, and INVENTORY MANAGEMENT.

PROFESSIONAL EXPERIENCE
June 1970 to Present: United States Army
Medical Services Corps, MEDDAC, Fort Bragg, CA
Chief of Logistics Division, San Diego Army Hospital (2/84–Present)
Primarily responsible for MATERIALS MANAGEMENT and all LOGISTICS SUPPORT at this 500-bed ARMY HOSPITAL with a staff of 1500. This involves the management of $8,200,000+ in equipment and supervision of five Branches: Materials, Property Management, Service/Utility, Medical Maintenance, and Housekeeping. Specific activities included everything from acquisition/storage, and distribution of Supplies to INVENTORY CONTROL of 1600+ Line Items; development of COST CONTROLS; administration of an annual $3,500,000 BUDGET. As Safety Officer, successfully maintained JCAH Accreditation and OSHA implementation. Major accomplishments: Increased Productivity; REDUCED ORDER/SHIPPING TIME 60% from five to two days; and SAVED $125,000+ in 1st year. This was achieved by instituting New Procedures for Inventory Control; by streamlining a Computerized Order Entry System; and reducing Excess User Inventory. Supervised 22 military/125 civilian personnel.

U.S. Army Readiness Region IX, Houston, TX
Chief of Medical Branch Assistance Team (3/82–2/84)
Activities centered on EVALUATION and INSTRUCTION of ARMY RESERVE MEDICAL UNITS in six MIDWESTERN STATES. Medical Team consisted of six Specialists, who prepared and delivered 20 Training Packages to 24 Medical Units. The Packages ranged from basic Organization of the Military System to Lifesaving and Emergency Medical Procedures. Duties ranged from preparing Reports/Proposals; advising Reserve Personnel on Training Requirements for obtaining a Military Occupation Specialty (MOS); to developing/implementing six LOGISTICAL TRAINING PACKAGES in Inventory, Requisition Procedures, Transportation Support, Supply Accounting, and Preventive Maintenance. AWARDED 'MERITORIOUS SERVICE MEDAL'.

Military Assistance Command Philippines, Joint Military Advisory Group
Senior Medical Supply Advisor (3/81–3/82)
Activities centered on providing MATERIALS and MANAGEMENT CONSULTING SERVICES to the MEDICAL DEPARTMENTS of Royal Laotian Military Branches. Duties ranged from programming, budgeting, and auditing of $2,000,000 in Medical Supplies for four 1200-bed Hospitals and eight Post Hospitals to LIAISON with the Medical Depot and Supply Division Chiefs and directly advising the Military Surgeon Generals of Laos. IMPROVED INVENTORY CONTROL by establishing New Procedures and implementing a Resource Management Training Program. Awarded 'JOINT COMMENDATION MEDAL'. Promoted to Lt. Colonel 2/82. Supervised two NCOs.

Another poised, compelling introduction that says a lot in just a single sentence.

MARY SMITH
45 Evansdale Drive, Anytown, State 00000 (555) 555-5555

Objective: To make an immediate positive contribution as a medical secretary, using in-depth knowledge of insurance, billing, and dealing with patients.

SUMMARY OF QUALIFICATIONS
- Responsible for all aspects of insurance billing and verification, i.e., Medicare, Medicaid, BC/BS, GHI, Metropolitan Empire, Senior Care, Primary, third-party, co-insurance and patient pay.
- Handled follow-ups for carders and patients, including checking on status of claims and correspondence.
- Computerized billing, including coding and input billings to customers.
- Maintained Accounts Receivable records and made daily deposits at bank.
- Scheduled appointments for up to thirty patients daily, involving patient contact.
- Functioned as a medical and surgical assistant: sterilizing equipment, preparing patients for surgery, ultrasound physical therapy, and developing X-rays.
- Demonstrated excellent attention to detail organization. Dependable. Work well independently or as part of a team. Able to bring effective solutions to complex problems. Willing to work hard and make contributions.

PROFESSIONAL DEVELOPMENT
FRANKLIN ASSOCIATES, Los Angeles, California   11/90–Present
Personal Secretary/Assistant (Part-time)

DAVID SWARM, Los Angeles, California   12/89–11/90
Medical Secretary/Podiatry Assistant
Activities centered around assisting 20–30 patients daily.

ELAINE O'BRIAN, Los Angeles, California   5/88–11/89
Medical Secretary/Podiatry Assistant
Handled all computerized billing and followed up with insurance companies when necessary.

ANN JAMES, Santa Barbara, California   4/86–4/88
Medical Secretary/Podiatry Assistant
Handled all correspondence for this busy office. Attended to 20–30 patients a day.

DONALD GRAHAM, Pasadena, California   8/84–2/86
Medical Secretary/Podiatry Assistant
Responsibilities shifted between front desk and assisting the doctor to administer to patients' needs.

MARIAN MURPHY, Pasadena, California   2/77–6/84
Medical Secretary/Podiatry Assistant
All billing was done manually. Patient contact. Functioned as receptionist.

EDUCATION
Compton Union High School, Compton, California   Graduated 1976—Academic Studies

HOBBIES
Travel... Horseback Riding... Cooking... Gardening... Fishing

References Furnished Upon Request

The inclusion of a seemingly unrelated early job actually
demonstrates important supervisory skills.

JOHN SMITH
45 Evansdale Drive
Anytown, State 00000
(555) 555-5555

Objective: Seeking a job as a health care professional working with the mentally and physically handicapped that will take advantage of my eight-plus years of experience in this area.

EMPLOYMENT EXPERIENCE
3/89–4/95   HARRISON DIAGNOSTIC TREATMENT CENTER, Fort Worth, Texas
Shift Supervisor (1992–present)
Responsible for overseeing the activities at this live-in facility for the profoundly mentally and physically ill. Supervised staff of ten Team Supervisors, Residential Counselors, and Housekeepers; managed quarterly and annual meeting to track patients' progress toward greater independence; assigned work schedules; maintained fire safety standards; collected data and completed administrative paperwork; worked with Program Supervisor to iron out staffing problems.

Residential Counselor (1991–1992)
Worked to establish daily goals, i.e., personal care/educational goals (reading, math, and writing). Supervised recreational activities; Med Certified and dispensed medications. Visited hospitals and conferred with physicians regarding medical procedures; and interacted with family members.

Housekeeper (1989–1991)
Responsible for maintaining a clean facility in order to pass federal inspections. This included outside, as well as interior, maintenance. Trained residents to assume some housekeeping tasks.

1986–1989   ALBERTSON JANITORIAL, Abilene, Texas
Contract Cleaner
Activities focused on fulfilling residential cleaning contracts at two major department stores. This involved direct supervision of small crews; worked with Field Manager and scheduled work.

EDUCATION
SAM HOUSTON COMMUNITY COLLEGE, Houston, Texas
Major: Graphic Arts, December 1984

LICENSE
Texas State CDL

A crisp, concise "Professional Profile" section gets the proceedings underway with a bang!

MARY SMITH
45 Evansdale Drive
Anytown, State 00000
(555) 555-5555

PROFESSIONAL PROFILE
- Reliable
- Organized
- Versatile
- Highly Motivated
- Excellent Communicative Skills
- Problem Solver

EXPERIENCE

5/95–Present   Returned from maternity leave as a part-time Staff Nurse in the Neonatal ICU, St. John's Medical Center, New Orleans, LA. Cited for "superior performance" on most recent evaluation.

12/91–11/94   Assistant Nursing Care Coordinator in the Neonatal ICU, St. John's Medical Center, New Orleans, LA. Named "best organized" team member in annual awards ceremony.

5/91–11/91   Staff Nurse in the Operating Room, St. John's Medical Center, New Orleans, LA.

3/88–5/91   Staff per diem in the Neonatal ICU, St. John's Medical Center, New Orleans, LA.
Ultra Care Agency.
Pediatric Home Care.
TPF Agency, Pediatric and Neonatal ICU.
St. John's Medical Center and Baton Rouge Hospital, New Orleans, LA.

11/80–3/88   Senior Staff Nurse in the Neonatal ICU, St. John's Medical Center, New Orleans, LA.

3/84–9/84   Staff per diem in Neonatal ICU, Baton Rouge Hospital, Baton Rouge, LA.

2/78–9/80   Staff Nurse in both Neonatal ICU and Pediatric ICU, Atlanta Children's Hospital, Atlanta, GA.

6/77–12/77   Staff Nurse in Medical-Surgical ICU, Jersey Shore Medical Center, Neptune, NJ.

EDUCATION:
Diploma in Nursing
Cincinnati School of Nursing, Cincinnati, OH.
Attended Alabama State University for Nursing Sciences.

ORGANIZATIONS:
Member of American Nurses Association
Louisiana State Nurse's Association

References Available Upon Request

The inclusion of multiple-language abilities is important in patient settings, and can often make all the difference for an entry-level applicant.

JOHN SMITH
45 Evansdale Drive
Anytown, State 00000
(555) 555-5555

OBJECTIVE
Seeking an entry-level position as a Nursing Assistant.

EDUCATION and SPECIAL TRAINING
MEDICAL AID TRAINING SCHOOLS, Los Angeles, California
Satisfactorily completed 122 hours of instruction, including 32 hours of supervised clinical experience as a NURSING ASSISTANT at Santa Ana Hospital Nursing Home, Los Angeles, CA. This involved bedside care, changing bed linens, following universal precautions, and other related procedures.

Qualified to care for Convalescents and Geriatrics, 3/95

Have completed the California State Facility Nurse Aide Certification program, enrolled in the California State RHCF Registry as of 4/95.

LATTONDA COMMUNITY COLLEGE, Long Beach, California
Assistant Physical Therapist program

Have completed 70 credits towards an Associate in Applied Sciences degree. Dates of attendance: 9/90–present.

Courses include: Introduction to Physical Therapy, Therapeutic Procedures I & II, Structural Kinesiology, Mobility, Fundamentals of Human Biology I & II, Pathology, General Psychology, Developmental Psychology, and Community Health.

EMPLOYMENT
8/92–Present   FAMILY HOME CARE, Santa Ana, CA
Personal Care Aide
Assist patients with daily activities; help patients prepare meals and assist in feeding; supervise the dispensing of medication; assist with ambulation, helping patients to move to different locations within the facility. Serve as an advocate for patients in order to maintain their social welfare benefits.

8/91–8/92   EXTENDED FAMILY CARE, Pasadena, CA
Personal Care Aide
Duties and responsibilities were same as those described above.

LANGUAGES
Fluent French and Spanish.

REFERENCES
Furnished upon request.

The applicant's ample relevant experience is outlined in an accessible, clearly organized way. Note the inclusion of applicable volunteer work from the college years.

JOHN SMITH

45 Evansdale Drive
Anytown, State 00000
(555) 555-5555

OBJECTIVE

To obtain a position as a Nursing Assistant in a facility where my significant experience interacting with patients would be an asset.

EXPERIENCE

4/94–Present   ALEXANDRIA CARE, Alexandria, Virginia
Home Health Aide

Assist elderly, ill, disabled, injured, or incapacitated clients in their own place of domicile. Perform a variety of home care services vital to those who would not be able to live at home without help. Duties and responsibilities are defined by individual needs of clients depending on specific disabilities and circumstances. This agency is affiliated with Alexandria Community Hospital.

11/92–6/94   COMPTON HEALTH SERVICE, Richmond, Virginia
Home Health Aide

Visited clients daily, working with a small number of patients at a time. Reported back to supervisors for explanations of the services needed by each client and discussed scheduled times of visits. This agency is affiliated with several hospitals in the metropolitan area.

12/91–11/92   SELF-HELP COMMUNITY SERVICES, Hopewell, Virginia
Home Health Aide

Provided clients with personal care tasks such as bathing and dressing, light housekeeping, shopping and preparing meals, transferring patients, range of motion, perineal care, check vital signs (T/P/R, blood pressure), oral care, and assisting with medications.
Achievement: Recipient of award for outstanding commitment to the Nassau County Health Care System.

1989–1990   BEVERLY THOMAS NURSING HOME, Lynchburg, Virginia
Assistant Cook

1985–1989   PEACEMOUNT PSYCHIATRIC CENTER, Emporia, Virginia
Assistant Cook

EDUCATION

ALEXANDRIA COLLEGE, Alexandria, Virginia

Successfully completed all course work necessary for certification as a Nursing Assistant, May 1994, including 100 hours of classroom and lab work and 35 hours of internship at Richmond Hospital.

VIRGINIA TECHNICAL COLLEGE, Richmond, Virginia

Computer Programming and Operation, 1979

The resume's emphasis on appropriate internships and public
speaking make the transition an understandable one.

JOHN SMITH 45 Evansdale Drive Anytown, State 00000 (555) 555-5555

OBJECTIVE

A career in sales where I may fully utilize my pharmaceutical expertise and interpersonal capabilities.

PROFESSIONAL EDUCATION

ST. MARY'S UNIVERSITY
COLLEGE OF MEDICAL AND HEALTH PROFESSIONS, Portland, Oregon
Bachelor of Science in Pharmacy—Sept. 1989 to Dec. 1993

ST. JOHN'S COLLEGE, Salem, Oregon
Participated in early admissions program, majoring in Business Administration,
Economics, and Voice and Diction—Jan. 1989 to June 1989

PROFESSIONAL EMPLOYMENT AND INTERNSHIPS

1994 Multnomah County Medical Center, Oregon City, Oregon
INTERN—CLINICAL MEDICAL TEAM
Prepared and presented case studies to assigned medical team, advising appropriate drug therapy.

1993 Drug Information Center, Multnomah County Medical Center, Oregon City, Oregon
INTERN
Researched and answered telephone inquiries from health professionals; interacted with
drug manufacturers when necessary. Documented all pertinent data.

1991–1992 Pritcherd Community Hospital, Department of Pharmacy, McMinnville, Oregon
PHARMACY INTERN
Prepared and filled prescription orders under the supervision of the Pharmacist. Totally responsible
for the IV admixture program, which included charting, timing, and preparing IVs.

1988–1989 OREGON STATE PHARMACY, Portland, Oregon
PHARMACIST'S ASSISTANT
Assisted in dispensing drugs and medications. Maintained all records: third-party
payments, patient profiles, and customer charges.

PUBLIC SPEAKING

Researched, prepared reports, and presented lectures on drugs to Pharmacy and Therapeutics
Committee of Multnomah County Medical Center for approval for the hospital formulary:
• Bumex (Bumetanide)—Peters Laboratories
• Wytensin (Guanabenz)—Forrest Laboratories

REFERENCES

Furnished Upon Request.

The targeted objective line ensures that this resume will stand out from the pack.

MARY SMITH
45 Evansdale Drive, Anytown, State 00000 (555) 555-5555

OBJECTIVE: Seeking a position as a Pharmacist with MaxWay Stores, where my experience and education would prove mutually beneficial.

PROFESSIONAL DEVELOPMENT
1983–Present: SAINT FRANCIS HOSPITAL CENTER, San Francisco, California

1986–Present: Senior Associate Pharmacist—Level B, Inpatient Services
Activities center on servicing the entire hospital consisting of fifty-five units. Primarily responsible for supervising the main pharmacy on the night shift and overseeing five pharmacists and two aides. This includes updating patient profiles, filling unit dose cassettes, screening drug interactions, correcting wrong dosages, obtaining doctor's approvals, dealing with other hospitals for purposes of restocking, implementing doctor's orders on ICU units, and troubleshooting a wide array of situations. Report directly to the head of the Pharmacy Department.

1983–1986: Staff Pharmacist—Outpatient Services
This required thorough knowledge of all outpatient procedures. Responsibilities included patient counseling, distributing narcotics, and fulfilling responsibilities as required.

1/83–5/83: HORTON'S DRUGS, San Mateo, California
Staff Pharmacist
Primarily responsible for filling Rx's, ordering inventory, restocking shelves, patient counseling.

8/81–5/82: BERKELEY PHARMACY, Berkeley, California
Jr. Pharmacist
Responsibilities included patient counseling, medicaid and third-party reimbursing, ordering inventory, OTC recommendations, and compounding prescriptions.

7/79–8/81: MATRON'S PHARMACY, Santa Cruz, California
Pharmacy Intern/Part-time
Activities included filling Rx's, compounding, patient counseling, medicaid billing, etc.

7/78–12/78: PETER'S CHEMIST, Monterey, California
Front-end cashier; assisted customers.

EDUCATION
UNIVERSITY OF CALIFORNIA SANTA CRUZ, Santa Cruz, California
College of Pharmacy
B.S. in Pharmacy, conferred 1981
Externship programs included: Saint Francis Hospital. Community Hospital: Drug Utilization Review in Antibiotics.

SAN FRANCISCO STATE COLLEGE, San Francisco, California, 9/74–6/77: Pre-Med Program

LICENSES
Pharmacy Licenses: California, 1987; Washington, 1982; Oregon, 1985

ASSOCIATIONS
California Pharmaceutical Association (active member)
American Pharmaceutical Association (active member)

LANGUAGES
Fluent in Spanish (written and spoken)

REFERENCES
Promptly available upon request.

A document's final line is often one of the most closely read. Take a look at the educational "punch" listed in the final line of this resume!

JOHN SMITH

45 Evansdale Drive
Anytown, State 00000
(555) 555-5555

WORK EXPERIENCE

4/95–Present   ALLENTOWN PHYSICAL THERAPY, Allentown, Pennsylvania
Physical Therapist Assistant
Staff Physical Therapist Assistant tending to patients with musculoskeletal injuries or problems in an orthopaedic private practice. Also render physical therapy in home care setting.

2/96–Present   BARTON & KEMPER ORTHOPAEDIC ASSOCIATION, Scranton, Pennsylvania
Dept. of Physical Medicine and Rehabilitation
Tend to patients with musculoskeletal injuries or problems in a physical therapy setting.

6/93–1/95   SCRANTON ORTHOPAEDIC AND SPORTS PHYSICAL THERAPY, Scranton, Pennsylvania
Physical Therapist Assistant
Staff Physical Therapist Assistant with responsibilities that included supervising cybex isokinetic exercise and testing, overseeing physical therapy aides, and rendering treatment to patients in an orthopaedic setting. Clinical instructor for physical therapist assistant students. Worked closely with physical therapists in developing and implementing therapeutic exercise programs.

5/93–6/93   NEW WARREN PHYSICAL THERAPY AND SPORTS REHABILITATION CENTER, P.C.
Physical Therapist Assistant
Tended to patients with orthopaedic or neurological injuries in a private practice setting.

6/90–4/93   MARTINEZ, O'BRIAN AND SEHALL, R.P.T., Sunburg, Pennsylvania
Physical Therapy Aide
Assisted with physical therapy for patients in a private physical therapy practice. Familiar with varied therapeutic modalities and procedures, such as ultrasound, electrical stimulation, and exercise instruction.

PROFESSIONAL ORGANIZATIONS
American Physical Therapy Association (APTA)
Affiliate Assembly of APTA

EDUCATION
HARRISBURG COMMUNITY COLLEGE (CUNY), Harrisburg, Pennsylvania
Associate Degree, Physical Therapist Assistant, 1993
G.P.A.—4.00   Dean's List

References Available Upon Request

The targeted objective and detailed coursework summaries combine
to make this resume a winner.

JOHN SMITH
45 Evansdale Drive
Anytown, State 00000
(555) 555-5555

OBJECTIVE: To obtain an internship at Parkway Medical Center in a physical therapy setting.

EDUCATION
9/92–Present   GREENSBORO COMMUNITY COLLEGE
Greensboro, Maryland

Major: Physical Therapist Assistant

Have completed 43 credits towards an Associate in Applied Science Degree.

Honors: Dean's List, Spring and Fall Semesters, 1993; Grade Point Average of 3.78

Certificate of Honor from York College in recognition for outstanding contribution and work as a mentor for the City University of New York Head Start for College Program

Certificate of Achievement for completion of the LaGuardia Allied Health Program

Relevant Coursework: Introduction to Physical Therapy, Biology I and II (Anatomy and Physiology), Functional Pathology, General and Developmental Psychology, Community Health, Aging and Health, Oral Communication, Mentoring.

EXPERIENCE
4/85–1/91

Construction Worker: Experienced in all phases of carpentry, roofing, street excavation, and concrete replacement. Worked as a laborer on the Con Edison Stream Enhancement Contract.

Peter's Roofing, Inc., Columbus, Ohio

Buildright Construction Corp., Hagerstown, Maryland

Jefferson General Contracting Corp., Dover, Maryland

ACTIVITIES
Volunteer tutor for the Greensboro College Biology Lab

Volunteer for Boys and Girls Club of Greensboro

Volunteered and helped raise money for Easter Seals of Greensboro

Organized and managed a softball team of disabled adults

Volunteer for Send a Kid Fishing Club of Greensboro

SKILLS
Perform well under pressure

Organizing and planning

Motivating others

Helping and being of service to others

REFERENCES
Available upon request

The resume's emphasis on particular categories of patients served emphasizes
points of commonality with the target employer.

John Smith

**45 Evansdale Drive
Anytown, State 00000
(555) 555-5555**

WORK EXPERIENCE

11/94–present   MURRAY MEDICAL CENTER
Physical Therapist Assistant (Per Diem)
Responsibilities included working in the Psychiatric Unit, Intensive Care Unit. Treatment of patients with cardiac conditions, AIDS, CVA, Parkinson's disease, and multiple sclerosis.

5/93–10/94   CATHOLIC NURSING HOME AND HOSPITAL
Physical Therapist Assistant (Per Diem)
Worked with Parkinson's disease patients, and neurologically involved patients, patients with knee and hip replacements, amputees, and patients with spinal stenosis and back problems. Application of modalities such as: ultrasound, electrical stimulation, massage, and gait training.

7/88–12/92   BENJAMIN R. FEINGOLD HEALTH CARE CENTER
Physical Therapist Assistant
Worked in a nursing home treating geriatric patients with a variety of diagnoses. Responsibilities included: completing various documentation, supervising and training Physical Therapy Assistant students, conducting rehab, making nursing rounds, training nursing staff, participating in interdisciplinary conferences, as well as MDS conferences, brace and wheelchair clinics, and in a Huntington's Unit.

CLINICAL EXPERIENCE

4/88–5/88   ORTHOPEDIC AND REHABILITATION DIAGNOSTIC TREATMENT CENTER
Queens, New York
Duties included: Treatment of patients with a variety of back problems. Use of cervical and pelvic traction, hydrotherapy, TENS, electrical stimulation, ultrasound, therapeutic exercise, and gait training.

1/88–2/88   VETERANS ADMINISTRATION HOSPITAL
Los Angeles, California
Duties included: Administration of various modalities, gait training, therapeutic exercise, and documentation.

7/87–8/87   CITY OF ANGELS MEMORIAL HOSPITAL
Los Angeles, California
Responsibilities were to work with Parkinson's disease patients, CVA patients, amputees, patients with hip and knee replacements, low back problems, arthritis, and patients with multiple sclerosis.

EDUCATION

LA HONDA COMMUNITY COLLEGE, La Honda, California
Physical Therapist Assistant

LICENSE   California State Certified Physical Therapist Assistant, exp. 10/31/98
LANGUAGES   Fluent in Spanish.
REFERENCES   Available upon request.

A powerful "Overview" summary gives insights on this applicant's experience base.

JOHN SMITH
45 Evansdale Drive
Anytown, State 00000
(555) 555-5555

OVERVIEW

Extensive clinical experience in comprehensive care of patients as individuals or families in areas of Pediatrics, Internal Medicine, Obstetrics, Gynecology, Human Behavior, Dermatology, and Diagnostic Radiology. Performance of 350 hours Emergency Room diagnosis and management of nonsurgical emergencies.

PROFESSIONAL EXPERIENCE

ROSALIA'S VASCULAR LABORATORY   1989–Present
Altoona, Pennsylvania
Responsible for supervision of day-to-day operations at the laboratory.

ST. MARY'S MEDICAL CENTER   1987–1989
Pittsburgh, Pennsylvania
Activities centered on noninvasive vascular diagnostic imaging techniques to support clinical diagnosis. Research included study of hypertension, diabetes, and cerebral vascular diseases.

Private Practice
COMMUNITY CARE MEDICAL CENTER   1983–1987
Caracas, Venezuela
Registration Number 155
Responsible for providing longitudinal health care to individuals and families as a Clinician. This included Diagnostic Radiology.

EDUCATIONAL BACKGROUND

ECFMG Certification   April 1991
Completion of requirements through FMG Exam Part I and Part II
Unrestricted License to Practice Medicine in Venezuela 1983

Licensing Prerequisite
CARACAS GENERAL HOSPITAL   2/82–3/83
Caracas, Venezuela
Rural area physician—Prerequisite for licensing

Rotating Internship
VALENCIA GENERAL HOSPITAL   1/81–2/82
Caracas, Venezuela
Intern—Departments: Internal Medicine, Surgery, Gynecology, Emergency Room, Pediatrics, Clinical Laboratory, and Psychiatry

Medical School
UNIVERSIDAD DE CARACAS   1975–1982
Caracas, Venezuela
Physician in Medicine and Surgery—Diploma

PERSONAL DATA

Married; Health Excellent; Permanent U.S. Resident.

REFERENCES

Personal and Professional References Available.

Note the inclusion of relevant computer skills near the end of
this resume—a powerful addition.

JOHN SMITH

45 Evansdale Drive
Anytown, State 00000
(555) 555-5555

CURRICULUM VITAE

POSTRESIDENCY EMPLOYMENT:

7/95–Present	Staff Physician
	SAN ANGELO Environmental & Occupational Health Inc.
	San Angelo, Texas 07094

7/92–7/95	Staff Physician
	San Saba Medical Center
	San Saba, Texas 10467

6/94–Present	House Physician (part time)
	San Antonio General Hospital
	San Antonio, Texas 11550

POSTGRADUATE MEDICAL TRAINING:

| PGY-3: 7/91–6/92 | Preventive and Occupational Medicine |
| | State University of Texas   Austin, Texas 11794 |

PGY-I & 2: 7/89–6/91	Internal Medicine
	Lubbock General Hospital
	Lubbock, Texas 11203

CLINICAL EXTERNSHIPS:

| 5/86–6/89 | Medicine, Pediatrics, and Emergency Medicine in various hospitals in Texas |

RESEARCH EXPERIENCE:

| 7/91–6/92 | Austin County Department of Health |
| | Division of Epidemiology |

| 1/86–4/86 | Austin City Department of Health |
| | Division of Epidemiology |

PROFESSIONAL CERTIFICATIONS:

Texas State Medical License   New Mexico State Medical License
Board Eligible: American Board of Preventive Medicine   Certified by ECFMG
Certified in Basic Life Support and in
Advanced Cardiac Life Support (ACLS)

EDUCATION:

Texas State University, Texas
Master of Public Health in Occupational Medicine, 1986
Texas State University
Doctor of Medicine, 1984

COMPUTER SKILLS:

dbase, WordPerfect, Harvard Graphics

ASSOCIATIONS:

American College of Physicians
American Public Health Association
Texas State University Alumni Association
American Heart Association
Medical Society of The State of Texas

Another resume with a powerful academic achievement withheld until the final line.

MARY SMITH
45 Evansdale Drive
Anytown, State 00000
(555) 555-5555

MEDICAL EDUCATION
MEDICAL COLLEGE, BREESON UNIVERSITY, Washington, D.C.
Doctor of Medicine
1978 to 1984

POSTDOCTORAL TRAINING
Residency
MADRID HOSPITAL, Madrid, Spain
General Surgery
1984 to 1985

Internship, Residency
BIRMINGHAM HOSPITAL AND MEDICAL CENTER, Birmingham, Alabama
Internal Medicine
July 1990 to June 1993

Fellowship
GREENVILLE HOSPITAL CENTER, Greenville, Alabama
Pulmonary Medicine
July 1993 to Present

ACADEMIC APPOINTMENTS
Staff Physician
MEDICAL COLLEGE, BREESON UNIVERSITY, Washington, D.C.
1986 to 1989

CERTIFICATION

ABIM, 1993	FMGEMS, 1990
FLEX, 1989	ACLS, 1993

LICENSURE
State of Alabama

RESEARCH WORKS
- A survey of prescribing habits among practitioners using Socitomebutol in the therapy of Tuberculosis. (Accepted for schematic presentation at 1995 ATS International Conference).
- Retrospective Study of utilization of PFTs in Medical Primary Clinic.

PROFESSIONAL SOCIETIES
Member, American College of Physicians
Member, American College of Chest Physicians

HONORS
1st Class Honors in Doctor of Medicine

The "Procedures Performed" summary offers all the relevant technical
detail in an accessible, easy-to-read format.

JOHN SMITH
45 EVANSDALE DRIVE
ANYTOWN, STATE 00000
(555) 555-5555

CAREER OBJECTIVE: Complete Internal Medicine Training, obtain Board Certification, and enter Primary Care Practice.

EDUCATION

UNIVERSITY OF ILLINOIS	DOCTOR OF MEDICINE—1990
ARIZONA STATE UNIVERSITY	DOCTOR OF MEDICINE—1981
UNIVERSITY OF LA MESA	MEDICINE—78/80
CHICAGO STATE UNIVERSITY	PREMED—77/78
PEORIA COMMUNITY COLLEGE	AA DEGREE, PREMED—1976

POSTGRADUATE SCHOOL OF TRAINING

BARTLETT MEMORIAL MEDICAL CENTER, Affil. CHICAGO UNIVERSITY MEDICINE, Illinois
PGY-1 Internal Medicine 7/91–6/92

Rotations:

July	Medical Floor
August	Medical Floor
September	CCU
October	RICU
November	Vacation
December	Medical Floor (Telemetry)
January	Medical Floor
February–June	Open

BILDROSE HOSPITAL, Affil. MONMOUTH STATE and UNIVERSITY OF ILLINOIS SCHOOLS OF MEDICINE, Illinois
Transitional Program (Straight Medicine)7/84–6/85

Rotations:

July	Radiology
August	Emergency Dept.
September	ICU
October	Infectious Diseases
November–February	Medical Floors
March–April	Pediatrics
May–June	CCU

PROCEDURES PERFORMED

Bone marrow aspiration and biopsy, abdominal paracentesis, lumbar puncture, subclavian line insertion, Swan-Ganz placement, central venous line placement, arterial line insertion, therapeutic thoracentesis, venipunture, peripheral line placement, arterial gases, endotracheal intubation, N.G. tubes, use of ventilators and ECG machines.

AWARDS/HONORS

Peoria Community College—Honor Student—eight semesters

PROFESSIONAL SOCIETIES

American College of Physicians—1991–1992

OTHER DATA

Bilingual in English and Spanish

Personal and Professional References Furnished on Request

A compelling combination of administrative and clinical
accomplishments makes this extended resume a winner.

MARY SMITH
45 Evansdale Drive, Anytown, State 00000 (555) 555-5555

PROFESSIONAL EXPERIENCE
Solo Private Practice:
FAMILY PRACTICE ORIENTED, Des Moines, Iowa **4/96–Present**
Deep clinical experience in comprehensive care of patients. Areas of interest: Pediatrics, Internal Medicine, Gynecology, Human Behavior, Dermatology.

Hospital Affiliation:
DES MOINES GENERAL HOSPITAL, Des Moines, Iowa **8/95–Present**
Family Practice Department
Assistant Attending Physician
Primary responsibilities focused on admitting private patients. Worked with and contributed toward goals set forth by department committees whose primary function was delivering high-quality health care.

Ambulatory Care Department—Family Care Network **8/95–3/96**
Contributed toward the implementation of a new outpatient health care delivery system. Worked closely with the administrative staff to expedite and coordinate all operations. Administrative functions included meeting with committees (on an ongoing basis) to review and adjust guideline practices and policies focusing on ways to improve services.

Solo Private Practice:
FAMILY PRACTICE ORIENTED, St. Louis, Missouri **8/92–7/95**
Extensive clinical experience in comprehensive care of patients as individuals or families. Areas of interest: Pediatrics, Internal Medicine, Obstetrics, Gynecology, Human Behavior, Dermatology, Emergency Medicine, office surgical procedures, and assisting in major surgical procedures.

Hospital Affiliation:
ST. LOUIS GENERAL HOSPITAL (Active Staff Member) **8/92–7/95**
Chairman, Family Practice Department **1/95–7/95**
Vice-Chairman, Family Practice Department **1/94–12/94**
Board Member of St. Louis Medical Associates (EMA)
Active participation in the formulation of a HMO and PHO, to provide a health care delivery system in association with the local hospital.

Training:
Family Practice—Postgraduate Training **7/89–6/92**

Solo Private Practice:
MEDICINE & SURGERY, Des Moines, Iowa **1978–1988**
Registration Number 884
Responsible for providing longitudinal health care to individuals and families as a Clinician and Surgeon. Experience in using noninvasive diagnostic imaging techniques to support clinical diagnosis. Extensive diversified experience while assisting in major surgical case and in the intrahospital follow-ups. Active teaching participation in internship programs. Performed over 840 hours emergency room diagnosis and management of surgical and nonsurgical emergencies.

DES MOINES SOCIAL SECURITY INSTITUTE, Des Moines, Iowa   **1979–1984**
House-Staff Officer—Surgeon Assistant (Surgery Department)
250-Bed Hospital (Social Security Health System)

DES MOINES SOCIAL SECURITY INSTITUTE, Des Moines, Iowa   **1977–1979**
House-Staff Officer—Surgeon Assistant (Surgery Department)
200-Bed Hospital of National Health System

LICENSES
State of Iowa, August 1992   State of North Dakota, 1992
State of Missouri, 1992   State of Nebraska, November 1991

EDUCATIONAL BACKGROUND
Board Certification (AAFP), July 10, 1992

Postgraduate Educational Experience:
Family Practice Residency Training
DES MOINES HOSPITAL, Des Moines, Iowa
PGY-I July 1989–June 1990   PGY-III July 1991–June 1992
PGY-II July 1990–June 1992   Chief Resident
FLEX Examination   December 1990
Successful completion of requirements of Part I and Part II
ECFMG Certification   March 1989
Completion of requirements through FMG Exam Part I and Part II
Unrestricted License to Practice Medicine in Colombia

Medical School:
IOWA STATE UNIVERSITY, 1969–1974
Physician in Medicine and Surgery—Diploma. Graduated January 16, 1976

AFFILIATIONS
• AAFP American Academy of Family Practice (Active Member), 1989
• AMA American Medical Association (Active Member), 1990
• AAFP American Academy of Family Practice of Iowa (Active Member)

PERSONAL
U.S. Citizen

REFERENCES
Personal and Professional References Available

The doctor's depth of experience with a learning-disabled patient
group is given appropriate emphasis.

JOHN SMITH
45 Evansdale Drive, Anytown, State 00000 (555) 555-5555

OVERVIEW
Extensive clinical experience in comprehensive care of patients in areas of Internal Medicine, Gynecology, Emergency Medicine, Psychiatry, Dermatology, Gastroenterology, ENT, Pediatrics, and Opthalmology. Performance of 1,000 hours Emergency Room diagnosis and management of nonsurgical emergencies.

PROFESSIONAL EXPERIENCE
COMMUNITY CENTER FOR CHILDREN WITH LEARNING DISABILITIES   7/90–present
Birmingham, Alabama
Activities focus on the treatment of children with learning disabilities.

HASTINGS DIAGNOSTIC LABORATORY   1984–1988
Montgomery, Alabama
Performed all medical tests, EKGs. Functioned as Lab Technician.

EDUCATIONAL BACKGROUND
FMGEM Certification   April 1991
Completion of requirements through FMG Part I (1991) and Part II (1990)

Unrestricted License to Practice Medicine in Mexico   1990

Licensing Prerequisite
ST. TERESA HOSPITAL   7/89–7/90
Managua, Nicaragua
Social Services
Departments: Internal Medicine, Surgery, Gynecology, Emergency Medicine, Psychiatry, Dermatology, Gastroenterology, ENT, Pediatrics, Ophthalmology, Traumatology.

Rotating Internship
HOSPITAL ZONA 11   7/88–7/89
Granada, Nicaragua
Intern
Departments: Internal Medicine, Surgery, Gynecology, Emergency Medicine, Psychiatry, Dermatology, Gastroenterology, ENT, Pediatrics, Opthalmology, Traumatology.

Medical School
UNIVERSITY OF LEON MEDICAL SCHOOL   7/84–7/88
Leon, Nicaragua
Physician in Medicine and Surgery—Diploma

Undergraduate College
CATHOLIC CENTRAL COLLEGE   1983
Kingston, Jamaica
Bachelor of Science

HOBBIES   Dancing, Tennis, Jogging, Reading.

PERSONAL DATA   U.S. Citizen

REFERENCES   Personal and Professional References Available.

A variety of college experiences are presented logically and directly,
and accompanied by relevant examination results.

MARY SMITH
45 Evansdale Drive, Anytown, State 00000 (555) 555-5555

Postgraduate Training	DETROIT METROPOLITAN HOSPITAL CENTER/DETROIT MEDICAL COLLEGE Detroit, Michigan Specialization: Internal Medicine PGY-1, 1995–1996
Medical Education	UNIVERSITY OF THE EAST—TOKYO MEMORIAL MEDICAL CENTER Tokyo, Japan Medical Degree, 1995
	SAN ANTONIO SCHOOL OF MEDICINE San Antonio, Texas Clinical Clerkship/Electives, 1994
College	YOKOHAMA UNIVERSITY, 1989–1991 Yokohama, Japan Bachelor of Science in Preparatory Medicine
	MARY IMMACULATE COLLEGE OF NURSING, 1988–1989 Tokyo, Japan
	FORT WORTH COLLEGE, Fort Worth, Texas, 1988 Completed 90+ credits, concentration in Biology. Cumulative average: 3.2
	PACE COLLEGE, San Antonio, Texas, 1985–1988 Completed 50 credits, concentration in Nursing. Cumulative average: 3.2
Medical Examinations	FLEX, Passed 12/86 (#03686-82810-8) ECFMG, Passed 2/94 (#3776515) MSKP, Passed 2/93 (Score: 42)
Personal Data	Date of Birth: May 7, 1968
	Birthplace: Tokyo, Japan
	Marital Status: Single
	Citizenship: United States
References	Personal and professional references available upon request.

The applicant's inclusion of brief, but relevant, business experience near
the end of the resume supports the candidacy effectively.

JOHN SMITH
45 EVANSDALE DRIVE, ANYTOWN, STATE 00000 (555) 555-5555

PROFESSIONAL EDUCATION

KILKENNY COLLEGE (CALLEN HOSPITAL), Kilkenny, Ireland, 1974—Diploma in Nursing

LITTLE ROCK COMMUNITY COLLEGE, Little Rock, Arkansas, 1988

PROFESSIONAL CERTIFICATION

Registered Nurse, Arkansas State License

Registered Nurse, Pennsylvania State License

PROFESSIONAL RECORD

PRIVATE DUTY NURSE at present

Private duty cases at Allentown Community Hospital, Allentown, Pennsylvania;
Lancaster County Hospital, Lancaster, Pennsylvania; Harris Hospital, Allentown,
Pennsylvania; Lebanon Central Hospital, Lebanon, Pennsylvania.

STAFF NURSE, Lancaster Community Hospital

O.R. NURSE, Dominican Hospital, Cincinnati, Ohio

STAFF NURSE, Sisters Hospital, Cincinnati, Ohio

NURSING SKILLS

Making accurate physical and psychological assessments of patients in medical and
surgical units, and in home settings. Nursing care for Oncology cases, Orthopedic
cases, terminal care, Parkinson's and Alzheimer's diseases. O.R. experience.

BUSINESS EXPERIENCE

TELLER, Fargo Bank, Fargo, North Dakota. Achieved "100% Club" accuracy award.

CLERICAL DUTIES, York Center for Child Development, Lancaster, Pennsylvania;
cited for "superior organization" by director of center.

PROFESSIONAL TRAINING

Critical Care Training, O.R. Training

Specialized GYN-Oncology

C.P.R.

Four powerful, understated paragraphs in "Medical Training" illustrate depth of experience.

JOHN SMITH
45 Evansdale Drive, Anytown, State 00000 (555) 555-5555

CURRICULUM VITAE

MEDICAL TRAINING: Chief Resident, Department of Psychiatry, 7/86–6/87
Resident in Psychiatry—7/83–6/87

- Fourth-year Chief Resident responsible for directing and overseeing work of 26 residents in program. Coordinate workshifts and on-call schedules; interview and review candidates for PGY I with Department Chairman.
- Rotations have included: Inpatient Psychiatry, Psychiatric ER, Internal Medicine, Neurology, Drug and Alcohol, Pediatrics, Child Psychiatry, Outpatient Clinic (including Day Hospital), Consult Liaison, Administrative Psychiatry, Community Psychiatry, and Forensic Psychiatry.
- Have served on-call duty in Psychiatric Ward, Psychiatric ER, and on other service Psychiatric consults.
- Serve as Lecturer in Psychiatric Education Rotation to first- and second-year residents—Topic: Paraphilia.

INTERNSHIP: University Hospital of Frankfurt, Frankfurt, Germany, 1982
Two months Medicine; two months Gynecology; two months Surgery.

EDUCATION: The University of Pisa Medical School, Pisa, Italy
1975–1983, Doctor of Medicine, January 1983

UNDERGRADUATE: Boston College, Boston, Massachusetts
B.A., Chemistry/Premed, 1975

EXAMINATIONS: ECFMG, passed July 1982 (#1854B)
FLEX, passed June 1984 (#00882)

LICENSURE: New York State #167612

COURSES/SEMINARS: Depression: Psychobiology, Psychodynamics and Therapy
Harvard Medical School, 1986

Psychiatric Depression
North Shore Center, Boston, Massachusetts, 1986
Have accumulated additional CME credits through Nassau County Hospital.

AFFILIATIONS: Member, American Medical Association

Administrative and supervisory skills are established early on—and dramatically.

JOHN SMITH
45 Evansdale Drive, Anytown, State 00000 (555) 555-5555

EXPERIENCE:

9/96–Present   *THE CITY OF BOSTON DEPT. OF HEALTH, Boston, Massachusetts*
Bureau of School Children and Adolescent Health
Public Health Nurse

My role as a P.H.N. encompasses case finding, referrals, follow-up, team functions, coordinating activities, providing a working relationship, and health preventive teaching. Other details include record review; teacher, parent and faculty conferences. Community liaison. Visits to medical room planned and unplanned. Annual regrading, home visits, record writing and review. Doctor sessions. Work in conjunction with school-based support team. Supervise assistants and health resource coordinators. Assess laboratory values. Presently assigned to seven schools.

8/91–8/96   *CRESTLINE NURSING HOME, Spencer, Massachusetts*
Head Nurse (R.N.)

Responsible for providing care to chronically ill patients in a 40-bed unit. Developed nursing care plans, form assessments. Administered medications and treatments, i.e., F/C insertion, finger-stick blood glucose, ADM 02 suctioning injections, etc. Interacted with staff and families.

1/91–8/91   *AUBURN HOSPITAL, Auburn, Massachusetts*
Staff Nurse (R.N.)

Responsible for general care of patients; handling 20–40 patients in a medical/surgical unit. Took histories, kept charts, administered medications, and prepared patients for tests and treatment. Maintained charts and medication records, etc. Interacted with staff and family. Frequently acted as Charge Nurse; responsible for entire function of unit. Functioned as a team leader, directing nurses' assistants.

2/80–1/81   *BAY STATE UNIVERSITY HOSPITAL, Salem, Massachusetts*
Staff Nurse (R.N.)

Worked 11pm.–7am. Supervised and directed nurses' assistants with the psychological, biological, and hygienic needs of the patients. Interacted extensively with doctors; actively involved in all unit functions. Oversaw 22 patients requiring total care and kept accurate documentation of all medication and treatment given in a medical/surgical unit.

ADDITIONAL EXPERIENCE:

4/85–Present   *AIR FORCE RESERVE, Powell Air Force Base (72AES)*
Flight Nurse, 1st Lieutenant
Inactive stand-by status

EDUCATION: *BOSTON COMMUNITY COLLEGE, Boston, Massachusetts*
A.A.S. in Nursing, June 1978
Major: Nursing   Minor: Physical Education

REFERENCES: Available upon request

Here, decades of distinguished experience are laid out in a direct, no-frills fashion. This works only if you've got the background to support it!

MARY SMITH
45 Evansdale Drive, Anytown, State 00000 (555) 555-5555

EXPERIENCE

ST. JOHN'S/LINCOLN HOSPITAL CENTER, Cleveland, Ohio
1990–Present: Associate Attending
1990–Present: Clinical Instructor in Radiology
Ohio State School of Medicine

DOWNSTATE MEDICAL CENTER, Cincinnati, Ohio
1989–1990: Assistant Professor, Clinical Radiology

ST. AGNES HOSPITAL, Mansfield, Ohio
1987–1989: Assistant Attending, Department of Radiology

COLUMBUS RADIOLOGY ASSOCIATES, Columbus, Ohio
1983–1987: Diagnostic Radiologist

INTERNSHIPS & RESIDENCIES

DAYTON HOSPITAL CENTER, Dayton, Ohio
1980–1983: Radiology Resident (Mixed)

SPRINGFIELD HOSPITAL CENTER, Springfield, Ohio
1978–1980: Urology Resident

HAMILTON COMMUNITY HOSPITAL, Hamilton, Ohio
1977–1978: Surgical Resident

NOVA SCOTIA GENERAL HOSPITAL, Halifax, Nova Scotia
1973–1974: Intern

EDUCATION

EDMONTON UNIVERSITY
School of Medicine, Edmonton, Alberta, Canada
1974: M.D.

EDMONTON UNIVERSITY
Edmonton, Alberta, Canada
1969: B.A.

MILITARY

UNITED STATES ARMY RESERVES
1965–Present: Captain

UNITED STATES ARMY, Medical Corps
1964–1967: Active Duty—Honorable Discharge
Rank achieved: Lieutenant

PROFESSIONAL SKILLS

Experience in general diagnostic radiology, including G.I. and angiography

PROFESSIONAL AFFILIATIONS

Member, American College of Radiology
Member, Ohio State Chapter of American College of Radiology
Member, Ohio Roentgen Society

CERTIFICATIONS

American Board of Radiology Certificate

MEDICAL LICENSES

State of Ohio; Dominion of Canada

REFERENCES

Available upon request

A direct, customized objective lays it all on the line. Very effective.

JOHN SMITH
45 Evansdale Drive, Anytown, State 00000 (555) 555-5555

OBJECTIVE
To obtain an On-Staff position as an RN at Mercy Hospital, where my experience,
devotion, and professionalism would benefit patients.

PROFESSIONAL DEVELOPMENT
8/92–7/93　　　　NURSING SERVICES, Boston, Massachusetts
LPN/Independent Contractor (per diem)

Actively assisted doctors on the Cardiac Intensive Care Unit, Surgical Unit, Medical Unit, and Neurosurgical Unit at St. John's Hospital.

Cardiac Care Unit: Procedures included a variety of coronary problems: postcatheterization, bypass,
abnormal chest pains (close monitoring), syncope episodes, etc.

Surgical Unit: Assisted with treating all patients admitted, suffering from everything from posttrauma,
stab wounds, stomach and ovarian cancer, cholelathiasis, and whipple procedures.

Medical Unit: Infections (septic), AIDS and GI bleeds.

7/88–8/92　　　　ST. JOHN'S HOSPITAL, Boston, Massachusetts
Registered Nurse/Staff—Neurosurgery
Intensive Care Unit (8/90–8/92)

Procedures: attended to many head and spinal cord injuries, brain tumors, aneurysms, laminectomy,
(AVMs) arterial venous malformations, craniotomy (VPs) ventricular periteneal shunts.

Clinical Care/Med-Surgical Unit (7/88–7/90)

As team player under the direct supervision of the acclaimed Dr. Sam Jaffe, assisted with patient care
after initial diagnosis and treatment. This involved stabilizing those close to neurodeficits and following up. Referring patients to therapy modalities and rehab setting to continue the recuperation process.

LICENSE
Registered Professional Nurse, State of Massachusetts, April 1988 (#404846)
(State Boards—February 1988)

EDUCATION AND PROFESSIONAL TRAINING
BROCKTON COMMUNITY COLLEGE, Brockton, Massachusetts
A.A.S. Nursing, January 1988 1/87–1/88

BOSTON MEMORIAL HOSPITAL
Nursing Internship
Assisted on Medical-Surgical floors. Attended to patients: took blood pressure, glucose finger sticks,
dressed wounds, etc.

References will be furnished in a timely manner.

The final line explains the applicant's situation in a way
the prospective employer can understand.

MARY SMITH
45 Evansdale Drive, Anytown, State 00000 (555) 555-5555

OBJECTIVE
To obtain employment as a Registered Nurse at ABC Company, where my experience and strong interpersonal abilities would prove a valuable asset and contribute to the overall success of the institution.

PROFESSIONAL EXPERIENCE
MELLON TRUST COMPANY, Miami, Florida (1994–1995)
Industrial Registered Nurse—Medical Department

Worked with medical staff of 15 in this clinic-like setting, including direct contact with four Physicians, six Registered Nurses, X-ray and lab technicians, and auxiliary office assistants. Responsibilities centered on delivering health care service for 8,000 employees (Smith Barney and Polk Davis) nationwide, and over 12,000 worldwide. Attended to individual needs of up to 120 patients a day. This involved: performing preliminary medical work-ups on applicants for preemployment physicals; routinely providing emergency care; treating illnesses (G.I., U.R.L., etc.) and minor trauma (sprains, burns, lacerations, etc.); in-depth evaluations of employees' physical condition after resuming work; administering extensive immunizations for foreign travel; competently providing vaccines and allergy injections.

PALM BEACH BURDINES, Palm Beach, Florida (1990–1994)
Industrial Registered Nurse

Worked with staff of 12 in this clinic-like setting for one of the world's largest department stores. This included aggressively providing medical attention to store employees and customers; dealing with emergencies as they occurred; when necessary, arranging for transfer of patients to nearby hospitals; effectively attending to minor illnesses and traumas; performing medical service on a courtesy call basis; preparing and assisting with preemployment physicals; completing employee evaluations for those returning to work; accurately completing all required paperwork.

DERMATOLIGIST'S OFFICE, Miami, Florida (1989–1990)
Registered Nurse

Professionally assisted M.D. with care of patients receiving treatment, and/or minor surgery for warts, cysts, dermabrasion, and hair transplants.

MIAMI HOSPITAL—EVAN CASTELL, Miami, Florida (1988–1989)
Staff Nurse—Psychiatric Division

Responsibilities centered on the care of patients. Prepared and dispensed medication for patients; observed, evaluated, and recorded routine and unusual behavior; assisted M.D.s with EST on patients; completed all required documentation; adeptly aided in organizing leisure and recreational activities.

EDUCATION
MEDICAL COLLEGE OF THE CITY UNIVERSITY OF MIAMI
Associate's in Applied Sciences—Registered Nurse (completed 64 credits)

PERSONAL
Returning from voluntary temporary retirement to raise family.

The "Professional Development" section outlines key experiences
and capabilities in an effective, direct manner.

MARY SMITH
45 Evansdale Drive, Anytown, State 00000 (555) 555-5555

OBJECTIVE
Seeking a position as a REGISTERED NURSE where my skills working with other medical personnel to assist patients and provide quality health care would be fully utilized.

EDUCATION
PITTSBURGH UNIVERSITY, Pittsburgh, PA
BACHELOR OF SCIENCE DEGREE IN NURSING (expected date of graduation: 1998)
Overall G.P.A.: 3.8   Minor: Computer Science

MCKEESPORT COMMUNITY COLLEGE, McKeesport, PA
A.A.S. in Nursing, January 1994
Curriculum included: Nursing Care Planning and Assessment, Fundamentals of Nursing, Medical and Surgical Nursing, Pediatrics, and Obstetrics G.P.A.: 3.0

LICENSES
REGISTERED NURSE—February 1994   LICENSED PRACTICAL NURSE—October 1993

CERTIFICATIONS
CPR—American Heart Association, expires January 1999
Infection Control and Barrier Precaution, May 1994
Advanced Pulmonary Assessment, June 1994
Respiratory Update Seminar, March 1995

PROFESSIONAL DEVELOPMENT
ALTOONA HOSPITAL MEDICAL CENTER, Altoona, PA 1/91–Present
Staff Nurse in Medical-Surgical Unit and Pulmonary Care Unit (2/94–Present)
Assist patients with all kinds of Medical and Surgical diagnoses. Give complete physical assessment, write care plans, educating patients as to procedures, etc. Assess skin conditions and apply proper preventive care and decubitus care.

Capable of handling patients on Heparin drip, Insulin drip, Dopamine drip, Dobutrex drip, and Morphine drip. Give blood-transfusions frequently and chemotherapy occasionally. Capable of maintaining central IV line, including permacath, hickman, subclavian, femoral and jugular catheter. Take care of different types of tubes: NGT, PEG, Foley catheter, colostomy bag, nephrostomy tube. Work with patients on ventilators, trach collar, ventimask, etc., in Pulmonary Care Unit. Confident in assessing patients' response condition and providing trach care and suction. F/T

Transporter (1/93–2/94)
Transported patients to Radiology Department for CT, Ultrasound, and Nuclear Medicine. Worked with OB/GYN patients, cardiac patients, and patients with bone fractures.

LASELL LANGUAGE SCHOOL, Pittsburgh, PA 7/90–1/91
Bilingual Instructor: French

LANCASTER COUNTY HOSPITAL, Lancaster, PA 7/90–1/91
Interpreter: Bilingual Responsibilities

ADDITIONAL EDUCATION
VERSAILLES MEDICAL UNIVERSITY, Shanghai, China 9/85–6/90
Completed 5 years of medical school curriculum: areas of Internal Medicine, General Surgery, Obstetrics, Gynecology, and Pediatrics. Received full scholarship and graduated with honors. Completed Medical Internship during the fifth year at the St. Denis and Chartres Hospitals.

PROFESSIONAL ORGANIZATIONS
Member of Pennsylvania State Nurses Association

The "Responsibilities" section benefits from the applicant's focus on interpersonal skills.

MARY SMITH
45 Evansdale Drive, Anytown, State 00000 (555) 555-5555

EDUCATION

1983–1986   MT. ELBERT COLLEGE, Gunnison, Colorado
              BSN Degree
              3.3 cumulative average

1981–1982   DENVER STATE UNIVERSITY, Denver, Colorado
              Liberal Arts

PROFESSIONAL EXPERIENCE

1986–Present   ST. JOHN'S HOSPITAL, Denver, Colorado
                 Title: Staff Nurse, RN
                 Cardiac Medical unit with telemetry
                 Cardiac Step Down unit
                 Medical/Surgical unit

Responsibilities: Charge person responsible for entire RN and subordinate staff on my shift, coordinator of patient care assignments. Participation in preceptor program, orientation and training of new personnel. Liaison between physician and patient. Coordination of health care departments to provide patient care, i.e., social work, physical therapy, home care. Participation in improving hospital policy and maintaining quality assurance. Planning, goal setting and implementation of patient care. One-to-one patient teaching. Teaching small groups of patients and family members. Participation in continuing education—programmed instruction, attending inservices. Assisting physicians with medical procedures. Pre- and postoperative care of patients.

SKILLS

Monitoring telemetry, taking and reading EKGs. Dressing changes, IV therapy, venipuncture certification, administering medications, hanging of blood and blood products, administration of chemotherapy, CPR certification.

INTERESTS

Aerobics, weight lifting, gourmet cooking, interior design.

References and transcripts available upon request

The use of a brief quote from a positive personnel evaluation
at the outset of the resume is a real plus.

JOHN SMITH
45 Evansdale Drive, Anytown, State 00000 (555) 555-5555

QUALIFICATIONS
REGISTERED NURSE
- Highly trained and experienced. Considered by supervisors to be an "excellent" nurse. (Personnel evaluation, January 1997.) Strongly motivated, provide quick accurate assessments, and work effectively and professionally with both hospital staff and with patients.
- Strong supervisory capabilities.
- Organized community fair, developed poster campaign, and worked closely with the health education committee at my current place of employment.

EDUCATION
Graduated College of Saint Francis with a Baccalaureate degree in Nursing in 1994. Member of the Student Nurses Association.
Recipient of NYS Regents Scholarship.

Graduated Saint Mary's High School, 1990.
Member of the National Honor Society.

EXPERIENCE
6/93–Present   GRACE MEMORIAL HOSPITAL OF THE SAM HOUSTON COLLEGE OF MEDICINE
Houston, Texas
REGISTERED NURSE
- Hired as a nurse's aide in my junior year of college. Stayed on after graduation as a Registered Nurse. Experienced in Neurology, Urology; general Med/Surg. nursing. After one year as a Registered Nurse I was put in charge of the Orthopedic and Vascular Unit comprised of 30 beds, and have been recommended for Senior Staff Nurse by both the Assistant Head Nurse and the Head Nurse.
- Involved with both the planning and implementation of eye testing, diabetes screening, and height and weight record keeping for the yearly health fair sponsored by the hospital.
- Conducting research on the fem pop. disease for the Society for Peripheral Vascular Nursing.
- An active participant in continuing education courses provided by hospital inservice and outside professional organizations.

3/92–5/93 COMMUNITY NURSING HOME, Gonzales, Texas
NURSE'S AIDE
- Praised for "consistently excellent work" and "commitment to patient welfare."

PERSONAL PROFILE
Age 24, Health excellent. From age sixteen until entering college, held several part-time jobs, as a bank teller, weekend manager in a San Antonio retail store, and in a bakery. These assignments allowed me to pay for much of my later education.

HOBBIES   Volleyball, swimming, needlepoint, aerobics

REFERENCES   Furnished upon request.

A strongly personalized objective outlines the applicant's
priorities in a compelling and positive fashion.

MARY SMITH
45 Evansdale Drive, Anytown, State 00000 (555) 555-5555

OBJECTIVE

To work as a community-based nurse. I thrive on the satisfaction of delivering quality, noninstitutional health care to meet the needs of individuals in their homes. The one-to-one nursing ensures total, individualized patient care. Experience: Agency Nursing, District Nursing. All experience was gained as a student nurse, community based where possible, i.e., District Nursing, Care of the Elderly, Obstetrics, Pediatrics, and Mental Health.

EXPERIENCE

June 1994–Present   MAGNOLIA NURSING HOME, Columbia, South Carolina
Position: Registered Nurse/Charge Nurse
Duties: Responsibility for delivering highest standards of care to 40 critically ill residents. Assign duties and supervise five nursing assistants, and one 1 L.P.N.

Oct. 1992–March 1994   HEARTHWAY PRIVATE NURSING HOME, Coventry, England
Position: Registered Nurse
Duties: In charge of 30-40 clients and a team of 3 nursing assistants. Clients ranging from light dependency to high dependency and dying. Worked closely with and supported relatives.

Jan. 1993–April 1993   PRINCE ALBERT GENERAL HOSPITAL, London, England
Position: Registered Nurse
Duties: Registered nurse working as part of a ward team. Experience: Medicine, Surgery, Children's and I.C.U. nursing.

March 1992–Sept. 1992   GLASGOW SERVICE HOSPITAL, Glasgow, Scotland
Position: Student Gynecology Nurse (Postgraduate)

April 1991–Dec. 1991   NEW GALLOWAY HOSPITAL, New Galloway, Scotland
Position: Registered Nurse
Duties: Worked as member of ward team in Medicine, Surgery, Orthopaedic Nursing, Care of the Elderly.

Jan. 1988–April 1991   QUEEN MARY'S HOSPITAL, Roehampton Lane, London SWI5 5PN, England
Position: Student General Nurse (Undergraduate).

EDUCATION

March 1992–Sept. 1992   QUEEN VICTORIA'S CHARITY HOSPITAL, Snowdon, Wales
Subjects: Gynecology and Women's Health (Postgraduate).
Areas Studied: General Gynecology Ward, Operating Theatres, Reproductive Medicine, Outpatient Clinic, Urology, Sexually Transmitted Diseases, Premenstrual Tension Clinic, Family Planning, Hirsutism Clinic, Endocrine Abnormalities Clinic, and Gynecology Unit, Royal Marsden Causerie Research Hospital.

Jan. 1988–April 1991   NEW GALLOWAY HOSPITAL, New Galloway, Scotland
Subject: General Nursing (Undergraduate)
Areas Studied: Medicine, Surgery, Gynecology, Obstetrics, Pediatrics, Orthopaedics, Operating Theatre, Care of the Elderly, Community Care, Plastic Surgery, Limb Surgery, Mental Health, Accident, and Emergency.

LICENSURE
Registered Professional Nurse, October 1994

PERSONAL
A person who can demonstrate:
Initiative and drive
A high degree of intellect and energy
Excellent communication and motivation skills

CERTIFICATION
Pennsylvania State Certification as Physical Therapist Assistant 4/13/93

The use of positive quotes in the opening section encourages interest and curiosity.
Just be sure you can attribute them properly during the interview!

MARY SMITH
45 Evansdale Drive, Anytown, State 00000 (555) 555-5555

SUMMARY OF QUALIFICATIONS
Excellent background, highly trained and experienced... Considered by supervisors to be a "superior" nurse...
Strongly motivated; work effectively with all other staff members... Able to "develop rapport with patients quickly
and easily."

PROFESSIONAL DEVELOPMENT
6/96–Present   ATLANTA HOSPITAL MEDICAL CENTER, Atlanta, Georgia
RN—Medical/Surgical Unit and Pulmonary Care Unit (6/94–Present)
Provide primary bedside nursing care, carrying out physician's instructions and helping with treatments. This involves administering medications, monitoring patients, and conducting physical assessments. Monitor life support
equipment. Record patient symptoms and reactions, chart progress.

Student Nurse Intern (6/93–6/94)
Assisted nursing staff with administering direct patient care on the Medical and Surgical Unit.

3/95–6/95   DR. DORIS CATLIN, D.D.S., Atlanta, GA
Dental Assistant
Assisted alongside the dentist during various procedures. Prepared for patients, i.e., cleaning, sterilizing, and disin-
fecting equipment; updating charts, and recording medical histories. Scheduled and confirmed appointments.

LICENSES AND CERTIFICATIONS
RN—Georgia State, September 1994
LPN—Georgia State, August 1994

IV Certification, March 1996
Advanced Pulmonary Assessment—Atlanta Hospital Medical Center, January 1994

CPR—American Heart Association, September 1994

EDUCATION
MACON COMMUNITY COLLEGE, Macon, Georgia
A.A.S. Degree in Nursing, June 1994
Overall G.P.A.: 3.0

TAYLOR COLLEGE, Augusta, GA
B.A. Degree in Communication Arts & Sciences, September 1990
Minor: Psychology
Courses included: Behavioral and Developmental Psychology

Prior Employment
Receptionist, KGO Network, Atlanta, Georgia
Sales Associate, Olivia's Department Stores, Atlanta, Georgia

REFERENCES
Available upon request.

Two part-time affiliations are outlined to maximum advantage here.
Note the inclusion of bilingual skills and patient teaching abilities.

Mary Smith
45 Evansdale Drive, Anytown, State 00000 (555) 555-5555

Objective: Seeking employment in an Outpatient/Clinical setting where I could use my skills to help address health needs within the community.

Employment History

Heath Medical Center, Pittsburgh, Pennsylvania 1/97–Present
LPN/Field Nurse
Conduct approximately 35 to 40 home visits a week for purposes of addressing medical concerns of a mostly elderly population. Report to and receive assignments through Heath Community Home Health Care Agency with five offices in the metropolitan area. Complete follow-up visits to address the following patient needs: diabetes, CHF, DAD, pneumonia, cancer, etc. Assist with caring for wounds, i.e., surgical wounds, decubiti, and venous stasis ulcers. Follow sterile techniques at all times. Provide practical teaching, informing patients of proper diets and disease pathophysiology. Multilingual (Spanish, French, English); provide translation as necessary.

Johnstown Hospital, Johnstown, Pennsylvania 4/96–Present
Licensed Practical Nurse
Presently working in a Family Practice Clinic prepping patients: taking vital signs, checking blood sugar prior to doctor's visit. Discharging of patients, administering immunizations, insulin, birth control injections, and other medications required through injections as ordered by medical doctor, including patient teaching. Assisting doctors with Pap smears, also administering PPD injections and PPD readings when appropriate, venipuncture, and some EKGs. Documentations: narrative translation PRN. Supervision by R.N volunteered—Johnstown Health Fair (9/96).

Education

Johnstown Community College, Johnstown, Pennsylvania
Practical Nursing Program—graduated May 1995
Coursework included:

•Anatomy	•Physiology
•Medication Administration	•Growth and Development
•Medical Surgery	•Pediatrics
•Pharmacology	•Psychiatry

Rotations:

Grace Memorial Hospital, Johnstown, Pennsylvania
Medical/Surgical
Studied and assisted with patient care. Performed as a Nurse under the supervision of instructor.

Lancaster County Hospital, Lancaster, Pennsylvania
Maternity/Pediatrics

Chester Community College, Chester, Pennsylvania
Geriatrics

Penn State University, Pittsburgh, Pennsylvania
Completed 23 Credits in Business Administration courses.

License

State of Pennsylvania, Licensed Practical Nurse, expires 8/98.

Additional Employment

Licensed Practical Nurse, Professional Home Care, Pittsburgh, Pennsylvania (12/95–6/96)
Unit Secretary, St. John's Hospital, Harrisburg, Pennsylvania (1991–1995)
Cashier, Lincoln Hospital, Lancaster, Pennsylvania (1988–1991)

An effective "what I believe" quote serves to define the applicant in
an instant—and set her apart from the competition.

MARY SMITH
45 Evansdale Drive, Anytown, State 00000 (555) 555-5555

"Happiness is the only good. The place to be happy is here. The time to be happy is now.
The way to be happy is to make others so."—Robert G. Ingersoll.

Professional Experience

1997–Present   EVEN TORREL HOSPITAL, Dallas, Texas
RN CN2
Responsibilities for patient teaching and training of nurses in hep-lock technique, venipuncture and access procedures, broviac, mediport types.
- *Access Nurse*
- *Member of IV Team*
- *Assist Chemotherapy Nurse*

1995–1997   FORT WORTH HOSPITAL, Fort Worth, Texas
Staff Nurse II
Worked as Charge Nurse evening and night shifts in Obstetrics, Gynecology, and Oncology wards.
Modalities:
- *Chemotherapy Treatments*
- *Invitro/Infertilities*
- *Abortions*
- *Venereal Diseases*
- *Post Parteros*
- *AIDS patients with children*

1992–1995   SAN ANTONIO CITY HOSPITAL, San Antonio, Texas
RN Star Nurse I/II
Participation in neurologic, neurosurgical, neurologic ICU, and rehabilitation cases.
- *Charge Nurse (all shifts)*
- *Earned Psychiatric Certificate 1982 and Critical Care Certificate 1983.*
- *Developed familiarity with various respirators, pumps, and intercranial calibration equipment.*

Educational Background

1983–Present   HUNTER COLLEGE, New York, New York
Regents External Degree
Specialized program of individualized study incorporating seminars, lectures, and courses from a variety of colleges.

1980–1982   CORPUS CHRISTI COMMUNITY COLLEGE, Corpus Christi, Texas
Associate of Applied Science in Nursing

Certifications   American Nurses Association: Medical Surgical Certificate, January 1989–December 1993

Affiliations   American Association of Critical Care Nurses (1983–1986)
Texas State Nurses Association (1982–Present)
National Student Nurses Association (1982–Present)
National Student Nurses Association
Association for Neurology and Neurosurgery Nurses (1982–1986)
Corpus Christi Community College Alumni Nursing Association (1982–Present)

References   Personal and professional references available upon request.

The emphasis on continuing education offers evidence that the
transition is a personal career commitment.

MARY SMITH
45 Evansdale Drive
Anytown, State 00000
(555) 555-5555

EDUCATION
SAINT CLOUD COLLEGE, Saint Cloud, Minnesota
Bachelor of Science Degree in Community Health, June 1992

GRACE HOSPITAL SCHOOL OF NURSING, Minneapolis, Minnesota
Diploma in Nursing, September 1990

LICENSURE
R.N. #142056-1 Minnesota

MILITARY STATUS
U.S. Air Force, July 1972–1989
Highest Rank: Major (Ret.)

ADDITIONAL EDUCATION
Childhood Injury Control, Minnesota HLTH-PRV-88.19, 1993 (4 hrs.)
Asthma Care, Minnesota HLTH-PRV-91-5, 1995 (12 hrs.)
Developmental Screening, Harriet Tubman Center, 1996 (28 hrs.)
HIV Counselor, CICASSIV- PRV 90-56, 1996 (25.2 hrs.)
Infection Control and Barrier, H93117, 1997 (3.5 hrs.)

PROFESSIONAL ASSOCIATIONS
• Grace Hospital School of Nursing, Alumni

• St. Cloud College, Alumni

• Phi Eta Phi Sorority, Inc.

• United Federation of Nurses, Local 523

• American Institute of Parliamentarians

Volunteer work, internships, and other relevant personal
experience are effectively highlighted here.

Mary Smith
45 Evansdale Drive, Anytown, State 00000 (555) 555-5555

OBJECTIVE
Registered Staff Nurse involving varied duties and responsibilities centering on administering medical care to ill and injured individuals.

EDUCATION
EVERETT UNIVERSITY, Everett University, Washington
Bachelor of Science in Nursing
(expected date of graduation—May 1995)
Courses: Nursing Concepts I & II, NSG Practicum I & II, Health
Assessment, NSG Implicit Drug Therapies, Microbiology & Lab, Human
Physiology & Lab, Nursing Nutrition.

INTERNSHIPS
1994–1995
BELLINGHAM COUNTY MEDICAL CENTER, Bellingham, Washington
Medical-Surgical Unit and Psychiatric Department

SEATTLE GENERAL HOSPITAL, Seattle, Washington
Medical-Surgical Unit

1994 (summer)
WASHINGTON STATE UNIVERSITY MEDICAL CENTER, Seattle, Washington
Worked under the guidance of Preceptor, helping to care for 5-7 patients, i.e., checking vital signs, etc.

EXPERIENCE
10/94–Present
DR. MORISSON BEADY, Niagara University, New York
Research Assistant
Obtained questionnaire data for research study "AIDS Knowledge Survey."

MT. RAINIER HOSPITAL, Olympia, Washington
Worked as a Volunteer.

CLINICAL EXPERIENCE
1993–1994
VETERANS ADMINISTRATION HOSPITAL, Vancouver, Washington
Medical-Surgical Unit and Orthopedics
Drafted Nursing-care plans and kept nursing notes while working on a one-on-one basis with patients.

SISTERS OF CHARITY HOSPITAL, Vancouver, Washington
Postpartum, Neonatal Care, and Critical Care
Tasks performed included: Catheterization, Dressing Changes, IV Monitoring, Distribution of Medications, Suctioning.

CHILDREN'S HOSPITAL, Vancouver, Washington
Pediatrics
Monitored vital signs, neurological checks, input and output data, completed assessment of patients, provided patient care as prescribed by diagnosis.

CERTIFICATION
American Association of Critical-Care Nurses, 5/94
American Red Cross/CPR

The applicant's "patient-first" outlook is supported by the summary of patient
education initiatives concerning medication and treatment.

JOHN SMITH
45 EVANSDALE DRIVE, ANYTOWN, STATE 00000 (555) 555-5555

A Registered Nurse committed to delivering quality care.

EXPERIENCE

3/95–1/96   SEATTLE NEPHROLOGY INC. (Seattle Kidney Center)
                  Seattle, Washington

Registered Nurse
- Provided one-on-one care to 6–10 ambulatory kidney patients on floor.
- Gained experience in operation of peritoneal and hemodialysis machinery.
- Interfaced directly with physicians, social workers, and dieticians in assessing patient condition and implementing effective treatment plans.
- Dispensed medication.
- Provided patients and family members with information regarding cause and effect of medication and explanations of treatment plans.
- Prepared monthly progress reports.
- Assisted in training new nurses.

7/94–2/95   REGIONAL GENERAL HOSPITAL
                  Glasgow, Scotland

Registered Nurse (Intensive Medical/Surgical Care Unit)
- Provided direct one-on-one care to critically ill patients, working intensive 12-hour, 7-day-a-week shift.
- Assessed and evaluated individual patient needs, reporting findings directly to physician.
- Gained familiarity with full range of intensive care equipment and machinery, including cardiac and hemodynamic monitoring, mechanical ventilation, and infusions.
- Dispensed medication.
- Provided patient's family members with information regarding patient's condition and treatment plans.

TRAINING

GLASGOW REGIONAL HOSPITAL, Glasgow, Scotland
Received Scottish Certificate of Registration as a Registered General Nurse, 1994.

Worked 40-hour week while attending classes full time. Received vital hands-on training in all hospital units, including ICU, OR, Pediatrics, Obstetrics, ER, and Psychiatry.

KIRKCALDY SECONDARY SCHOOL, Kirkcaldy, Scotland
Graduated with Leaving Certificate, 1990.

EXAMS TAKEN

Passed CGFNS (Commission of Graduates of Foreign Nursing Schools) exam, 1994

LICENSURE

Washington State Registered Nurse (Granted 1995).
Registration # 378464-1

REFERENCES

Available upon request.

The applicant's domestic licensure is addressed early on, ensuring that the prospective employer will be able to resolve an inevitable early question about a candidate whose education is with an overseas institution.

MARY SMITH
45 Evansdale Drive, Anytown, State 00000 (555) 555-5555

SUMMARY

Trained and experienced. Considered by supervisor and physicians to be "capable" and "strongly motivated," and to possess "ability to interact effectively with patients, colleagues, and supervisors."

LICENSES

The University of the State of Michigan/Education Department
Registered Professional Nurse, April 1991
• Limited Permit to practice as a Registered Professional Nurse issued November 1990.

Commission on Graduates of Foreign Nursing Schools
• Fulfilled necessary requirements for C.C.F.N.S. examination and passed both Nursing and English language proficiency sections, including comprehensive examinations in the following areas: Medical, Surgical, Psychiatric, Pediatric, and OB/GYN in 1990.

PROFESSIONAL EXPERIENCE

1/91–Present   DETROIT GENERAL HOSPITAL, Detroit, Michigan
Registered Nurse—Medical/Surgical Floor
Activities focus on delivery of patient care through the nursing process of assessment, planning, implementation, and evaluation. Direct and guide patient teaching; assess physical, psychological, and social dimensions of patients; plan formal written plans of patient care; utilize all available resources in planning care and consult with supervisors, physicians, and family when necessary; implement technical and clinical aspects of care; administer medication; prepare patients for OR and assist with postoperative care. Completed hospital-sponsored training and certified as B.C.L.S.

EDUCATION

ROME SCHOOL OF NURSING, Rome, Italy
Nursing Diploma, 1989

Coursework included:
• Administrative Nursing Service
• Nursing Research
• Population & Family Planning
• Community Health Nursing
• Health Assessment
• Philosophy & Ethics of Nursing
• Oriental Medicine
• School Health Nursing

Overall G.P.A.: 3.25

OUTSIDE INTERESTS

Youth Hostel . . . Travel.

REFERENCES

Furnished upon request.

A good example of an extended resume that holds attention from beginning to end.
Note the appealing "Personal Summary" at the beginning of the document.

JOHN SMITH
45 EVANSDALE DRIVE, ANYTOWN, STATE 00000 (555) 555-5555

OBJECTIVE
Seeking a position as a Registered Nurse in a hospital setting that would benefit from my experience, and where my continued professional development would be enhanced.

PERSONAL SUMMARY
Demonstrated professionalism and accountability... Able to organize and provide effective nursing care... Compassionate... Desire to help others... Reliable... Good communication skills... Exhibits stamina... Able to follow directions... Working either independently or as a team member, can focus on the problem and direct the solution... Leadership skills... A good role model... Able to supervise the activities of others.

QUALIFICATIONS SUMMARY
Registered Nurse... 10 + years' experience at three VA Medical Centers, in Miami and on the West Coast, also at a private hospital in Miami, and at the Department of Health in Puerto Rico.

NURSING SKILLS SUMMARY
Able to exercise sound clinical judgement... able to assess situations quickly while making rounds... diabetic reactions/glucometer checks/IV lines... ventilators and respiratory diseases/nebulizer treatment via tracheostomy... able to perform various health screenings, tests, and procedures... able to handle paperwork such as patients' charts... instruction of individuals on preventive health care... take vital signs/temperature/pulse/blood pressures, etc.

PROFESSIONAL DEVELOPMENT
VA MEDICAL CENTERS
8/88–5/93
VA MEDICAL CENTER, Miami, Florida   (7/91–5/93)
Registered Nurse
Functioned as a Charge Staff Nurse; completed comprehensive reports on each patient; informed incoming staff of any and all problems: infiltrations, insomnia, etc.; followed policies and procedures; was aware of and able to deal with patient behavioral patterns due to hospitalization diagnosis; offered emotional support to patients; formulated written nursing care plans; implemented physicians' orders; performed in emergency situations.
Accomplishment: Staff of the Month

VA MEDICAL CENTER, Milwaukee, Wisconsin   (7/90–7/91)
Registered Nurse
This unit was a 40-bed General Medicine Ward. Worked to improve patient care; resolved patient care problems by utilizing procedures for safety, comfort, and prompt recovery; directed activities of other team members; set and reset priorities based on changes in patients' conditions; interacted with Doctors, Medical Students, Nursing Students, Social Workers, Dieticians, and other personnel; participated in multidisciplinary discharge planning.
Accomplishment: Special Contribution Award

VA MEDICAL CENTER, Loma Linda, California   (4/91–7/91)
Registered Nurse
Provided primary bedside nursing care for the General Medical Unit. This included changing dressings, cleaning wounds, administering medication, accounting for narcotics, starting intravenous fluids, and monitoring medical equipment. Recorded patients' symptoms and reactions and charted their progress regarding medication and/or course of action prescribed by the attending physician; aided with assessing needs of patients and developed treatment plans; supervised aides, orderlies, and L.P.N.s individually in their duties.

VA MEDICAL CENTER, Miami, Florida   (8/88–4/91)
Registered Nurse (Night Shift)
Worked on the Respiratory Ailments Step-Down Unit, Intermediate Floor, and assisted with all procedures.
Charge duties: While making rounds, administered medications, checked ventilators, tracheostomy care, and vital signs. Worked with morning shift for purposes of overall direction of patient care.

PERRIN HOSPITAL, Tampa, Florida   (1987–1988)
Registered Nurse—Medical Surgical Unit

DEPARTMENT OF HEALTH, Florida, Milwaukee, Wisconsin   (1978–1985)
Registered Nurse
Activities centered on family planning. This health center provided a wide variety of services. Problem isolation and goal setting. Worked closely with physicians; extensive educational services were provided to patients regarding their options. Utilized audio/visual aides. Completed pap-smears; screened patients. After integration with public health sector, oversaw the activities at the various clinics: hypertension, OB/GYN, diabetes, TB.

LICENSES
• Office of Regulation and Certification of Health Professionals of Milwaukee, Wisconsin
• Registered Nurse

Completed all continuing education courses to maintain Registered Nurse License:
• Delivery, Management, and Documentation of Patient Care (1991)
• Mandatory Reviews (1991)
• Immobility: Facing the Challenge for Critical Care Nursing (1990)
• Emergency Nursing Review (1988)
• Development Management and Documentation of Patient Care (1988)
• The Nurse as an Educator of Diabetic Patients (1988)

NATIONAL COUNCIL LICENSURE EXAMINATION FOR REGISTERED NURSES, New York State—passed boards, July 1993

EDUCATION
MIAMI STATE UNIVERSITY, Miami, Florida
Associate Degree in Nursing

References Furnished Promptly Upon Request

A "personalizing" quote leads off the resume and underlines
the applicant's commitment to her work.

MARY SMITH
45 Evansdale Drive
Anytown, State 00000
(555) 555-5555

"All have but one entrance into life."—Anonymous

EDUCATION

MASON MEDICAL CENTER, STATE UNIVERSITY OF KANSAS
HEALTH SCIENCE CENTER AT SALINA, Salina, Kansas
Bachelor of Science in Nursing

MIDWEST COLLEGE, Scoll City, Kansas
Major: Prenursing

EXPERIENCE

1/88–Present   HUTCHINSON HOSPITAL MEDICAL CENTER, Hutchinson, Kansas
Staff Nurse—Labor and Delivery Departments
* *Antepartum assessment, evaluation, and care of normal gravid women.*
* *Antepartum evaluation and care of high-risk, preterm, and complicated pregnancies.*
* *Care of patients during normal or preterm complicated labor and delivery.*
* *Assisting medical doctors in the operating room during Caesarean sections, hysterectomies, and tubal ligations.*
* *Postpartum care of patients after normal deliveries, Caesarean sections, tubal ligations, and hysterectomies.*
* *Postpartum care of patients experiencing medical complications such as Disseminated Intravascular Coagulation (D.I.C.), H.E.L.L.P. Syndrome, and preeclampsia prior to admission to Intensive Care Unit.*
* *Postpartum education on breastfeeding to lactating women.*
* *Postpartum infant care to new mothers.*

8/86–11/87   WICHITA COUNTY HOSPITAL CENTER, Wichita, Kansas
Staff Nurse/Charge Nurse—Neonatology Department
* *Patient care of the premature infant in the Intensive Care Unit.*
* *Patient care of the high-risk infant experiencing such complications as drug withdrawal, hydrocephalus, diabetic mothers, low Apgars, Down's Syndrome, and meconium aspiration.*
* *Patient care of infants requiring special observation or having infections such as sepsis, HIV-positive mothers, serology-positive mothers, tuberculosis-positive mothers, and chorioamnionitis.*

LICENSE NUMBER: 390113-1

A good example of an extended resume that holds attention from beginning to end.
Note the appealing "Personal Summary" at the beginning of the document.

JOHN SMITH
45 EVANSDALE DRIVE, ANYTOWN, STATE 00000 (555) 555-5555

EDUCATION
Aurora University, Aurora, Illinois
B.S., May 1995, Nursing

Springfield College, Springfield, Illinois
B.A., May 1991, Psychology

PROFESSIONAL EXPERIENCE

11/96–present
CEDARS HOSPITAL, Child Psychiatric Unit
Staff Nurse
Assess primary patient design and implement individualized care plans
Attend interdisciplinary meetings
Attend family sessions
Collaborate with other disciplines

6/95–6/96
VISITING NURSE SERVICE, Springfield, Illinois
Assess family interaction
Physical assessment of patient
Instruct in parenting, infant care. Use and implement plan of care to meet patients'/families' goals
Coordinator of care—introduce other disciplines to help clients attain their goals and to maintain optimal health

OTHER WORK EXPERIENCE

5/93–10/93
UNITED SALES, Springfield, Illinois
Sales
Contacted potential clients to utilize additional services offered by the New York Telephone Company.

10/90–7/92
TAKAHASI INC., San Francisco, California
Sales Associate, Receptionist, Collections
Arranged sales displays
Worked on individual basis with customers
Corresponded with customers
Pursued delinquent accounts

5/89–9/89
AMTRAK RAILWAY, San Francisco, California
Reservation Agent

(Above part-time positions helped to defray full-time college expenses.)

STUDENT EXPERIENCE
As a student I completed an internship with the Visiting Nurse Service of Springfield. I practiced in the field of Maternal-Child.
Assessed mother-child interactions.
Devised and implemented care plans.
Carried my own case load.

PERSONAL DATA SS# 113-50-6856

LANGUAGE
Speak and write French, Spanish, and Japanese.

REFERENCES
Furnished upon request.

The "Community Service" heading, near the end of the resume, offers
an excellent opportunity for this applicant to set herself apart.

MARY SMITH
45 Evansdale Drive, Anytown, State 00000 (555) 555-5555

CAREER OBJECTIVE
To complete a categorical residency in Internal Medicine, and to write the Board examinations; to do fellowship in Geriatrics, to pursue a career in Academic Medicine/Research, and to practice medicine.

PROFESSIONAL EXPERIENCE
UCLA MEDICAL CENTER, West Los Angeles, California   7/98–Present
Fellow

Project Associate in Geriatric Clinic determining mini mental status and functional status assessment. Elderly Abuse Project.

MEDICAL & DENTAL OFFICE, Los Angeles, California   8/96–7/98
Medical Assistant

Drawing blood, collecting samples, and sending them to laboratory (Metpath). Working in conjunction with Doctor to detect/identify abnormalities in laboratory test reports. Performing blood sugar tests for diabetic patients, occult blood screening tests for high-risk patients, and PPD screening tests. Administering influenza vaccinations; documenting test results in patient records. Microscopic examination of vaginal secretions for yeast (KOH preparation), Trichnmonas; Performing blood CBC, ESR, and urine dipstick and microscopic examinations.

MEDICAL OFFICE, Pasadena, California   12/94–3/96
Medical Assistant
Duties primarily as listed in above position.

SERVICE HOSPITAL, Bombay, India   10/93–7/94
Medical Officer
Provided medical treatment to approximately 50 patients daily, including medicinal, surgical, and gynecological procedures.

COMMUNITY HOSPITAL, Bombay, India   6/92–9/93
Resident (Department of Plastic Surgery)
Involved in management of outdoor and indoor patients, including provision of assistance in surgical procedures; attending teaching rounds and clinical pathological conferences.

EXAMINATIONS
California State—FLEX, June 1998   Presently awaiting results.

FMGEMS (Jan. 1987)   Basic Science: 78; Clinical Science: 79

M.B.B.S. (June 1982)   Bombay University (Dow Medical College)

COMMUNITY SERVICE
Rendered services in rural area (1992–1994), teaching people about good health habits and providing them with general medical assistance.

LICENSURE/ASSOCIATIONS
Registered Medical Practitioner (Bombay Medical & Dental Council, #5211-S); Adult CPR (AHA); Child & Infant CPR (AHA); Member of Young Medicose Organization.

There's a virtue in getting right to the point. Here, the applicant's straightforward
educational and career path is laid out in a direct, powerful fashion.

MARY SMITH
45 Evansdale Drive, Anytown, State 00000 (555) 555-5555

EDUCATIONAL BACKGROUND

WESSON HEIGHTS HOSPITAL, Wesson, Vermont
Currently PGY 2—Internal Medicine, under Director Harold Pickson, M.D.;
Anticipated Completion of Residency: 6/98
First Year Residency (PGY 1): 7/95–6/96
Second Year Residency (PGY 2): 7/96–6/97

ROSA UNIVERSITY SCHOOL OF MEDICINE, Kingston, Jamaica
Medical Doctorate 1991–1993

UNIVERSITY OF VENEZUELA, Maracalbo, Venezuela
School of Medicine 1989–1991

UNIVERSITY OF MIAMI, Miami, Florida
College of Pharmacy 1984–1987
B.S. in Pharmacy

UNIVERSITY OF FLORIDA AT TAMPA, Tampa, Florida
Major: Prepharmacy 1982–1984

BISCAYNE UNIVERSITY, Biscayne, Florida (Summers)
Major: Prepharmacy 1982/83/84

PROFESSIONAL EXPERIENCE

ST. PETERSBURG PHARMACY, St. Petersburg, Florida   7/86–4/87
Position: Pharmacist

KECK PHARMACY, Lauren, South Carolina   1982/83/84
Position: Pharmacist (Summers)

ALEX PHARMACY, Macon, Georgia   1/80–7/81
Position: Pharmacy Intern

HIGH SCHOOL PHARMACY, Portland, Maine   9/79–12/79
Position: Pharmacy Intern

VETERANS ADMINISTRATION HOSPITAL, Portland, Maine   1/79–6/79
Position: Pharmacy Intern

EARNST PHARMACY, Montgomery, Alabama   8/79–1/80
Position: Pharmacy Extern

MEDICAL CENTER, GOLDS HOSPITAL, Portland, Maine   5/78–8/79
Position: Pharmacy Extern

LICENSURE
Examinations

FLEX: ID #5600017 (Completed in Vermont) 6/87
ECFMG: Certificate #368-321-6   7/86/1/85
English Exam: No. A 7284 (Valid Indefinitely)   1/87

Licenses

Registered Pharmacist: Maine—Certificate #24418
Florida—License #R 118360

REFERENCES

Personal and Professional References Available Upon Request.

Note the inclusion of information about times when the
applicant filled in successfully for her supervisor.

Mary Smith
45 Evansdale Drive, Anytown, State 00000 (555) 555-5555

OBJECTIVE

To obtain a supervisory position, consistent with my experience as a Respiratory Therapist, where I could be most helpful in delivering quality health care to patients.

PROFESSIONAL DEVELOPMENT

11/90–Present   SAN DIEGO MEDICAL CENTER, KOSTER DIVISION, San Diego, CA
Respiratory Therapist
Administration and monitoring of all diagnostic and therapeutic modalities within the services scope of practice. Provide respiratory support to all patients. As per physician orders, initiate, monitor, and adjust parameters on mechanical ventilators, the use of oxygen and humidification therapy, perform spontaneous ventilatory assessment, etc. Able to fill in for Supervisor (have done so on nine occasions, with superior results); responsible for other therapists when necessary. Work three days per week.

7/91–Present   THE SANTA ANA HOSPITAL MEDICAL CENTER, Santa Ana, CA
Registered Respiratory Therapist (7/91–Present)
Administer all forms of routine and advanced respiratory therapy modalities and techniques; perform invasive and noninvasive techniques of a diagnostic and therapeutic nature in accordance with department policy and procedure; interact with all medical personnel to resolve patient care issues, critical care independent of supervision; assist with clinical instruction of new employees when requested by supervisor; participate in department safety program; and develop and maintain a high level of customer service. On-call/per diem basis.

Ward Clerk (4/86–10/90)
Activities centered on assisting the Nursing staff with receptionist, clerical, messenger, and transporter responsibilities and other duties as required. More specifically, this involved developing and maintaining a high level of customer service, i.e., good oral communication and interpersonal skills for dealing with patients, families, visitors, and staff. Basic clerical skills, good planning and organizational skills.

10/90–2/92   LOS ANGELES CATHOLIC MEDICAL CENTER, Los Angeles, CA
Respiratory Therapist
Experienced in Pediatric, ICU, Neonatal ICU, all areas of adult care.

EDUCATION

SANTA MONICA COMMUNITY COLLEGE, Santa Monica, CA
Completed all requirements of Respiratory Therapist Program, June 1991.

SIMMONS COLLEGE, West Los Angeles, CA
Studying toward B.S. degree
Curriculum includes upper-level Science courses.

SANTA BARBARA COMMUNITY COLLEGE, Santa Barbara, CA
A.A.S. Degree in Business/Marketing, January 1988

HOBBIES

Cycling, Travel, Photography

The inclusion of personal references and contact information adds weight and authority.

JOHN SMITH
45 Evansdale Drive, Anytown, State 00000 (555) 555-5555

EDUCATION

Rome University, School of Medicine, Rome, Italy
Graduation date: December 1987
Degree Received: M.D.
Exams Passed:

FMGEMS, January 1992	Scores: 78–80
FLEX, June 1993	Scores: 77–80

EXPERIENCE AND QUALIFICATIONS

July 1996–Present
Surgical Intern
Dallas Hospital's Orthopedic Medical Center, affiliated with Texas State
College of Medicine

July 1995–July 1996
Internal Medicine
St. John's Hospital, Grand Rapids, Michigan

July 1994–July 1995
Internal Medicine
University of Wisconsin

LICENSE

State of Texas, No. 125-024425
Issued July 1, 1994

PERSONAL DATA

Sex: Male... Place and Date of Birth: Rome, Italy, April 4, 1964... Status: Permanent Resident of the United States... Alien Number: A284 77 581.

REFERENCES

Harold Grossman, M.D..
Chairman, Dept. of Surgery
Dallas Hospital
Dallas, Texas
555/555-5555

John Cartera, M.D.
Program Director, Orthopedic Surgery
Surgical Residency Program
Dallas Hospital
Dallas, Texas
555/555-5555

Marion Peters, M.D.
Chairman of Orthopedic Surgery
Dallas Hospital
Dallas, Texas
555/555-5555

The inclusion of personal references and contact information adds weight and authority.

John Smith
45 Evansdale Drive
Anytown, State 00000
(555) 555-5555

MEDICAL BACKGROUND
Internal Medicine
Residency: 1993–1996; Augusta Hospital and Medical Center, Augusta, Maine
Experienced in Invasive Critical Care and Endoscopic procedures.
Trained in Emergency Room management as surgical and medical resident.
ACLS Certified

General Surgery
Residency: 1991–1993; Augusta Hospital and Medical Center, Augusta, Maine

Otolaryngology: 1988–1990; M.S. University of Rome, Italy
Extensive training in Otolaryngology

Internship: 1986–1987; M.S. University of Rome, Italy

QUALIFICATIONS
M.S.:   Master of Surgery—Otolaryngology
D.L.O.:   Diploma in Otolaryngology
M.B.; B.S.: Bachelor of Medicine and Bachelor of Surgery

LICENSURE
Licensed in the states of Maine, New Hampshire, Massachusetts, and Vermont for the practice of Medicine and Surgery.

AFFILIATIONS
Associate Member, American College of Physicians
Member, American Medical Association

DATE AVAILABLE
July 1996

REFERENCES
Available upon request.

Diverse skills acquired in a foreign country form the basis of a solid
appeal for U.S. placement. Note the strong "Overview" that boils
the resume down to a single paragraph for busy readers.

JOHN SMITH
45 Evansdale Drive, Anytown, State 00000 (555) 555-5555

OVERVIEW
Extensive clinical experience in areas of Pediatrics, Internal Medicine, Obstetrics, Gynecology, Human Behavior, and Dermatology. Intensive diversified experience in surgery, including seven-year period serving as Surgeon Assistant in
two major hospitals. Responsibilities encompassing preoperative care, assisting surgeons in the operating room,
postoperative care and intrahospital follow-up. Active teaching participation in Internship Programs. Performance of
over 840 hours Emergency Room diagnosis and management of surgical and nonsurgical emergencies.

PROFESSIONAL EXPERIENCE
SAN LUIS POTOSI SOCIAL SECURITY INSTITUTE 1989–1994
San Luis, Mexico
House-Staff Officer—Surgeon Assistant (Surgery Department)
250-Bed Hospital (Social Security Health System).

MEXICO CITY GENERAL HOSPITAL, Mexico 1987–1989
House-Staff Officer—Surgeon Assistant (Surgery Department)
200-Bed Hospital of National Health System

Private Practice
MEDICINE & SURGERY, Mexico 1988–1998
Registration Number 884
Responsible for providing longitudinal health care to individuals and families as a Clinician and Surgeon. Experience in using
Noninvasive Diagnostic imaging techniques to support clinical diagnosis since 1985.

EDUCATIONAL BACKGROUND
ECFMG Certification March 1998

Unrestricted License to Practice Medicine in Mexico 1988

Postgraduate Experience
SACRED HEART HOSPITAL, Mexico 4/86–4/87
Physician—Rural Area—Prerequisite for licensing.

Rotating Internship
GUADALAJARA GENERAL HOSPITAL, Mexico 1/85–12/85
Intern
Departments: Internal Medicine, Surgery, Gynecology, Emergency Room, Pediatrics, Clinical Laboratory, and Ophthalmology

Medical School
VERA CRUZ UNIVERSITY, Vera Cruz, Mexico 1979–1984
Physician in Medicine and Surgery—Diploma

PERSONAL DATA: Married; Health Excellent; Permanent U.S. Resident.

REFERENCES: Personal and Professional References Available.

TOXICOLOGIST

JOHN SMITH
45 Evansdale Drive
Anytown, State 00000
(555) 555-5555

A highly qualified, energetic, detail-oriented clinical toxicologist

PROFILE

Highly regarded professional (and winner of six peer awards) focused on maintaining excellent record of attendance/punctuality in the workplace...Flexible, easy to work with, able to interact with people of varying backgrounds...Loyal, trustworthy individual, eager to establish long-term relationship with an employer.

EDUCATION

TEXAS STATE, Houston, Texas
M.S. in Pharmaceutical Sciences, January 1988
Specialization: Toxicology

Theoretical background: Analyzing Composition of Substances; Ascertainment of Drug Content; Laboratory samples using instrumentation such as H.P.L.C., T.L.C., Gas Chromatography–Mass Spectrometry, and I.R.

B.S. as Pathologist Assistant, September 1983

Studies included: Assisting Pathologists in Autopsies; Histological Preparation of Surgical and Biopsy Specimens; Obtaining Medical Histories of the Deceased.

EXPERIENCE
1976–Present

HOUSTON GENERAL HOSPITAL, Houston, Texas
Position: Respiratory Therapist
Procedures and duties include arterial blood gas analysis, endotracheal intubation, assisting surgeons in the insertion of tracheotomy tubes; breathing treatments for patients with various lung disease states, e.g. asthma, emphysema, pneumonia, etc. Quality control analysis on blood gas machines and ventilator maintenance.

REFERENCES

Supplied promptly upon request.

Another customized personal summary that instantly gets
the resume moving in the right direction.

John Smith
45 Evansdale Drive, Anytown, State 00000 (555) 555-5555

Committed to making an immediate positive contribution as a nursing
training and development specialist at Clevis Medical Center.

ACADEMIC PREPARATION
M.S. Health Care Management and Urban Policy, New School for Social Research, San Francisco, California, 1995
B.S.N. Nursing, Mary Mount College, San Francisco, California, 1978
B.A. Psychology, Mary Mount College, San Francisco, California, 1975
B.A. Sociology, with a certificate in Social Work, Mary Mount College, San Francisco, California, 1975
Academic Honors: Sociology Award for Academic Achievement, 1975; Dean's List, 1974-1978.

NATIONAL CERTIFICATIONS
Certified Critical Care Nurse (CCRN)
Certified Emergency Nurse (CEN)
Trauma Nursing Core Course (TNCC)
Emergency Nurses Pediatric Core (ENPC)
Advanced Cardiac Life Support (ACLS)
Pediatric Advanced Life Support (PALS)

ADDITIONAL TRAINING
Certified Nonviolent Crisis Intervention Instructor: National Crisis Prevention Institute, 1994
Forensic Investigation, St. Louis University, St. Louis, Missouri, 1992
Small Business Development Program, Hofstra University, Uniondale, New York, 1990
Effective Speaking & Human Relations, American Language Academy, Los Angeles, California, 1989 Recipient of two awards for achievement.

PROFESSIONAL NURSING EXPERIENCE
ST. FRANCIS NURSING HOME OF MARIN, San Rafael, California
1/95–Present: Administrative Nursing Supervisor
Act as the chief trainer and administrator for the 11:00 P.M. to 7:00 A.M. shift at this 432-bed skilled nursing facility. Supervision of the entire nursing staff: RNs, LPNs, CNAs. Conduct ongoing clinical training of the staff. Interact with resident physicians, handle emergencies, and make clinical assessments; communicate with local hospitals; initiate staff meetings to standardize patient care, increase morale, troubleshoot; initiate cost-effective measures; consult on new product purchases. Knowledgeable of MDS plus.

ST. AGNES HOSPITAL, Fresno, California
6/93–6/94: Nursing Unit Supervisor Assistant—Emergency Department
Coordination of patient care, interdisciplinary communication. Responsible for the management, evaluation, clinical development of Nursing Staff. Participation in Continuing Quality Improvement projects. Patient education and client satisfaction.

ST. JUDE'S MEDICAL CENTER, San Francisco, California
9/91–5/93: Nursing Education Specialist—Emergency and Ambulatory Services
Primarily responsible for the theoretical and clinical development of the emergency and outpatient nursing staff.
Involved in the design, coordination, and conduction of Specialty Care Orientation. Member of the Corporate Emergency Services Committee. Co-chairperson of Policy and Procedure Committee for Emergency Services. Participation in Continuing Quality Improvement projects. Involved in development and offering of NYSNA-approved CEU programs including review program for Certification in Emergency Nursing (CEN) and Critical Care Nursing (CCRN).
  * Guest lecturer for the CMC Emergency Medical Services Institute
  * Recipient of Excellence in Education award, 1994.

MARIN COUNTY MEDICAL CENTER, San Rafael, California
2/90–1/91: Critical Care Instructor
Developed formal orientation program for all critical care nursing areas. Responsible for compliance with JCAHO regulations for staff development in the critical care areas.

SAN FRANCISCO GENERAL HOSPITAL, San Francisco, California
9/88–3/89: Radiology Nurse for Special Radiology Procedures
Assisted with invasive radiology procedures, conducted patient teaching, assisted with follow-up physical exams for patients who completed their course of radiation therapy.

3/85–9/88: Critical Care Clinician
Clinical resource nurse for ICU, CCU, intermediate/special care units, recovery room, and emergency department. Co-coordinator of AACN sponsored critical care certification programs. Development of policies and procedures.

3/85–9/88: Critical Care Supervisor/per diem

WESTWOOD HOSPITAL, West Los Angeles, California
1/84–3/85: Critical Care Float
3/82–1/84: Assistant Head Nurse/Coronary Care Unit
6/81–3/82: Staff Nurse—Cardiothoracic Unit

FRANCISCAN CHILDREN'S HOSPITAL, Palo Alto, California
3/79–6/81: Assistant Head Nurse/Medical ICU

NORTHERN CALIFORNIA MEDICAL CENTER, Palo Alto, California
7/78–2/79: Staff Nurse/Coronary Care Unit

BUSINESS EXPERIENCE
PRIMED INTERACTIVE, San Francisco, California
7/94–Present: Nursing Consultant
Act as a resource for market trends within the health care industry and health care education. Additional activities center on creating innovative solutions to the challenges of educating all health care professionals. Innovative methods utilize a technologically sophisticated approach to advanced principles of adult learning. Participated in promotional videos. Consultant reports included in corporate publications designed to generate investment revenues.

DETAIL ACTION, INC., San Rafael, California
9/90–9/91: President
I conceived of this small business venture, researched the market, developed a business plan, secured investment funding, and developed a client base. Solely responsible for the day-to-day operation, sales, advertising, marketing, development of promotional material, budgeting, and monitoring of customer satisfaction.

INTERNATIONAL PROMOTION SERVICES, Burbank, California
3/89–10/89: Professional Nurse Recruiter
Screened applicants for an in-depth assessment of their qualifications, attitudes' and ability to meet immigration requirements. Performed background checks on credentials and references. Planned successful marketing strategies, created promotional materials. Developed screening tools, matched nursing skills to hospital-client requirements. Sales, client satisfaction, CSHO documentation.

PROFESSIONAL AFFILIATIONS
American Association of Critical Care Nurses
Emergency Nurses Association, Nassau/Queens Chapter Secretary, 1995
International Association of Forensic Nurses
National Nursing Staff Development Organization
National Association of Female Executives
National Gerontological Nursing Association

At the top of the resume, a single summary sentence makes bold
(and effective) use of the first-person pronoun.

MARY SMITH
45 Evansdale Drive, Anytown, State 00000 (555) 555-5555

I am a skilled triage/emergency room nurse with a demonstrated record of management experience.

EDUCATIONAL BACKGROUND

ATLANTIC UNIVERSITY, New Haven, Connecticut	Bachelor of Science in Nursing, 1983
ST. MARY'S UNIVERSITY, Scranton, Pennsylvania	Associate Degree in Accounting, 1979
HARRISBURG COLLEGE OF MEDICINE, Harrisburg, Pennsylvania	Paramedic School at Jacobi, 1984

Student Nurse: Boston Catholic Hospital, Boston, Massachusetts
Worked under Senior Emergency Room Preceptor.

PROFESSIONAL EXPERIENCE

LEADER'S MT., Fall River, Massachusetts   **9/87–Present**
Paramedic

BOSTON HOSPITAL MEDICAL CENTER, Boston, Massachusetts   **1/87–Present**
Emergency Department Staff Nurse (Night Charge Nurse)
Responsibilities for overseeing all nurses, nurses' aides, and fluxing personnel, dispensing medications, and coordinating patient treatments in Adult Emergency, Pediatric, and Triage. Additionally, acting as Preceptor for new Emergency Department nursing personnel.

ST. JOHN'S HOSPITAL, Harrisburg, Pennsylvania   **9/86–Present**
Instructor/Allentown Paramedic   **10/80–2/85**
* Coordinate and teach A.C.L.S. and C.P.R. courses

MIAMI HOSPITAL CENTER, Miami, Florida   **4/86–1/87**
Adult Emergency Department Staff Nurse
E.R. treating 600 to 800 patients daily
Rotations: Cardiac/Trauma, Triage, Chargeperson, Asthma Room

JACKSONVILLE COLLEGE HOSPITAL, Jacksonville, Florida   **2/85–3/86**
Emergency Department Staff Nurse
Rotations: Cardiac/Trauma, Triage, GYN, Asthma, Pediatric

READING HOSPITAL-EASTERN MEDICAL CENTER, Reading, Pennsylvania   **5/77–10/80**
E.M.T.
Functioned as an E.M.T. on mobile unit and in relief capacity in the Emergency Department.

R.N., B.S.N., C.E.N., E.M.T.-P

PROFESSIONAL ASSOCIATIONS
• American Nurses Association • Massachusetts State Nurses Association
• American Association of Critical Care Nurses • Emergency Nurses Association

CERTIFICATIONS
• Registered Nurse, Massachusetts State • Certified Emergency Nurse
• Pennsylvania Paramedic • American Heart Association C.P.R. and A.C.L.S. Instructor
• Pennsylvania E.M.T. Instructor

REFERENCES
Personal and professional references available upon request.

The final line offers important information on U.S. certifications.

MARY SMITH
45 Evansdale Drive, Anytown, State 00000 (555) 555-5555

An experienced triage nurse with a personal commitment to
delivering the highest possible standard of care to patients

EDUCATIONAL BACKGROUND
TRENTON UNIVERSITY, Trenton, New Jersey
Attended Comprehensive Courses: Med-Surg., Pediatrics, OB, Psychiatry (1981)

NURSING SCHOOL OF WARSAW, Warsaw, Poland
Completed Four-Year Diploma Program Specializing in Med-Surg.

ZYRARDOW HIGH SCHOOL, Warsaw, Poland
Academic Studies

PROFESSIONAL EXPERIENCE
11/82–Present   PATTERSON COUNTY GENERAL, Patterson, New Jersey
Triage Nurse
- *Primary responsibility for operation of Triage Office.*
- *Handling and evaluating vital problems through telephone triage or immediate in-person assessment of patients' nursing care needs.*
- *Decision making: ordering house calls and ambulances, extensive phone work.*
- *Routine duties including dressing changes, blood sugar testing, multiple injectable treatments, blood pressure screening.*
- *Prenatal health advisement, pregnancy interviewing, HMO setup.*
- *Responsible for maintenance of emergency crash carts' updating and requisitioning injectable drugs and supplies for entire center.*
- *Maintaining high standards of supportive care.*

9/81–10/82   PATTERSON MEDICAL GROUP, Patterson, New Jersey
RN
- *Responsible for performing activities involved in Regular Nursing Stations.*
- *Administering various treatments, vaccinations, etc.*
- *Working on rotating scheduling in Dermatology, E.N.T., Surgery, E.K.G., and Pediatric Departments.*

1975–1981   COTTAGE GROVE HOSPITAL, Newark, New Jersey
RN
- *Primarily employed as Staff Nurse; worked in Medical-Surgical Ward and Recovery Room.*
- *Assessing and providing general nursing care needs.*
- *Administering scheduled medications and treatments.*

1973–1975   IRENE BURTON (Private Practice), Trenton, New Jersey
RN
- *Performance of various testing and nursing procedures, such as venipuncture, E.K.G., physiotherapy, blood pressure testing.*
- *Preparing patients and assisting surgeon with minor surgical procedures.*

RELEVANT DATA
New Jersey State Registered Professional Nurse; CPR Certified; Up-to-date New Jersey State Registration.

The objective, and virtually all of what follows it, has been
tailored to match an existing job description.

MARY SMITH
45 Evansdale Drive, Anytown, State 00000 (555) 555-5555

OBJECTIVE

Seeking a full-time position where my recent experience working with computers and superior typing skills would be fully utilized.

SUMMARY OF QUALIFICATIONS

Computer Skills: WordPerfect 5.1, Lotus 1-2-3, Windows; type 45 wpm.

Secretarial Skills: Experienced in various aspects of office work. Detail-oriented person with strong organizational abilities. Accurate and reliable.

Interpersonal Skills: Highly regarded by colleagues and supervisors for friendliness, hard work, and the ability to learn new procedures. Work effectively with patients and co-workers alike.

EMPLOYMENT EXPERIENCE

RHINELANDER UNIVERSITY HOSPITAL—WISCONSIN
UNIVERSITY MEDICAL COLLEGE, Rhinelander, Wisconsin   1989–1992
Certified Nursing Assistant
Responsibilities centered on total patient care: Checking blood pressure, vital signs, etc. Worked with other health care professionals. Completed a variety of paperwork: updating patient charts, i.e., observing and recording signs and symptoms, etc.

VISITING NURSE SERVICE of WAUSAU, Wausau, Wisconsin   1986–1989
Nursing Assistant
Activities centered on a number of short-term assignments, assisting with patient care. Trained to work in any unit of a health care facility. Completed documentation of patient care, i.e., keeping records and completing forms, etc.

CERTIFICATION

Wisconsin State Certified Nursing Assistant

EDUCATION

CREATIVE CAREERS CENTER, Milwaukee, Wisconsin   1996
Personal Computer Specialist/Certificate
WordPerfect 5.1, Lotus 1-2-3, Windows
Internship: Red Cross of Milwaukee
Performed general secretarial/clerical duties.

HAVEN BUSINESS SCHOOL, Chicago, Illinois   1992–1993
Secretarial Studies
Studies included: Legal and medical typing (knowledge of medical terminology), WordPerfect 5.0, medical billing, reports.

ASSOCIATION

Member—Notary Public, National Notary Association

References Furnished Upon Request

Appendix
Help!

The following resume firms supplied talent, insights, and/or sample resumes for this book. If you're looking to develop a superior resume for your job search within the health care industry, and you feel you need one-on-one attention as you craft your resume, these are the people to call.

Executive Resume Career Marketing Services
P.O. Box 79
Cedar Brook, NJ 08018-9998
1-800-563-6359

Resume Center of New York
15-23 120th Street
College Point, NY 11356
718/445-1956
718/445-1296 (fax)

Resumes by James
102-30 Queens Boulevard
Forest Hills, NY 11375
718/896-6856
718/544-3300 (fax)

Index